GO
for It

———

GO
FOR IT:
GET ORGANIZED

Sara Gilbert

MORROW JUNIOR BOOKS / NEW YORK

Printed in the United States of America.

1 2 3 4 5 6 7 8 9 10

Library of Congress Cataloging-in-Publication Data
Gilbert, Sara D.
Go for it : get organized / Sara Gilbert.
p.   cm.
Includes index.
Summary: Suggests organizational methods to budget your time.
ISBN 0-688-08852-X.—ISBN 0-688-09619-0 (pbk.)
1. Teenagers—United States—Time management—Juvenile literature.
[1. Time management.   2. Life skills.]   I. Title.
HQ796.G495   1990
640′.43′0835—dc20   89-13765   CIP   AC

*For Joan—
with thanks as well to Bill*

CONTENTS

AUTHOR'S NOTE

When I was a student, people asked me how I managed to go to school, help care for my home, edit the school paper, play in the band, sew and garden, join several clubs and youth groups, do volunteer work, have a social life, and still get good grades.

Later, people asked me how I could possibly keep house, care for my family, lead the PTA, travel, and write books.

Today, people ask me where I find the time to hold a full-time job, meet family responsibilities, participate in various community groups, have a social life, and write books.

The answer: I'm organized.

Good organization gives me time, energy, and "smarts." I learned how to get organized by reading, paying attention, observing, and practicing—by trying different systems and adapting them to my own particular needs at the time. I still do that; each time I reorganize, I try to make things simpler.

Since I've written thirteen books for young people and know how much they want to do and how disorganized they often feel, I thought it might be helpful to pass on some of my own experiences in getting organized. The idea is not to get you to do things the way *I* do them but to get you started on the way to finding the organizational method that's good for *you*.

I've had times—and still do—when the process of organizing itself had me trapped, so I hope you'll figure out that *good* organization is the kind that frees you.

I've also learned that organizing—my tasks, my ideas, my

dreams—helps me clarify what it is I'm getting organized for; it helps me get clear about my goals, about knowing not just how to go for something, but what to GO for. So I hope you'll come away from this book with some of that, too.

PREFACE

STOP!

Before you GO and read this book about how to get organized, here's your first tip. It's about how to read this book.

Oh? You already know how to read a book? You begin at the beginning and work your way through to the end? Or perhaps you're one of those speedy types who reads only the end and assumes you can figure out what went before.

With either system, you're doing it the hard way.

Here's the easy, GO-for-it way—the simple, orderly, step-by-step way that lets you get the most out of the time and effort you put in.

Begin at the beginning, yes—by reading through the Contents and the first few pages. In any book, this front matter will tell you, in short—and usually simple—form, what the book is *going* to tell you.

Then take a look at the whole picture by thumbing through the book, reading only the big type and dark printing. These highlights will tell you more about what the book is going to tell you. In this book, you'll find preview-summaries at the beginning of each chapter, and reviews at the end. Using such helps and highlights makes it easier for your mind to sort through all the material in order, without carrying around a lot of excess baggage.

Once you've gotten an overview, go back to the beginning and go through the entire book step by step.

As you read about how to get organized and GO for it, you'll also find lots of chances to "Try It" with self-tests and practices that let you try out the GO principles. So before you start, find a pad and pencil, and keep them handy.

Now—GO for it: first your overview, and then step by step through the simple system.

GO
for It
____

INTRODUCTION

SOS!

This is the traditional seafaring emergency call to "Save Our Ship!"—to rush first aid to a sinking vessel. On land—and in daily life—it stands, simply, for "HELP!"

Do you ever feel the need to send out an SOS? To holler "help" because you just have too much to do and your life is just too confusing to manage? Do you ever feel as though you're paddling upstream in a leaky canoe? That's not surprising if you're like most people your age.

This book responds to that SOS with an S–O–S of its own: a Simple, Orderly, Step-by-step system for applying first aid to your range of activities. It will help you to stop frantically bailing out water long enough to get organized and GO for whatever goals shimmer on your horizon.

What's more, this S–O–S rescue system fits *your* life and style; it's not one whose mastery will only add to the things you have to learn each day or require you to squeeze your life into its rules. It calls for no special skills or equipment, yet you can apply it to any situation—major or minor, urgent or long-term—that you face.

When we learn first aid, we learn that the emergencies we're preparing for can come in almost any form, from a cat scratch or a broken finger to a train wreck or an earthquake. Yet a first-aid instructor teaches a simple group of basic procedures that can apply to any emergency. You'll learn the same kinds of procedures here.

In a first-aid course, the instructor teaches you to survey

the scene and the victim quickly, seek help, and survey the victim again *before* you act.

Then you learn what actions to take, step by step, one piece at a time. And to help you remember what you've learned, the instructions are condensed into short lists and keywords. That way, you're likely to be able to function almost automatically when faced with a real-life emergency—when you may hold a life in your hands.

GO for It: Get Organized puts "first aid" at your fingertips, too—first aid for *your* life.

In case that sounds too melodramatic, how about:

> "You can do everything you have to, ought to,
> and *want* to. You can do it well and still have time
> left over if only you'd . . . *get organized!*"

How many times have you heard that? Too many.

Yet how many times have you been shown *how* to organize? Too few.

Oh yes. Your English teacher tells you how to organize a paragraph or a paper, and in chemistry you're told how to organize an experiment.

But organization itself? A system that can help you plan anything from a picnic to a future—help you achieve even the most impossible goals or untangle the most complicated situation? People tell you to "go for it"—but they don't tell you *how*. Besides, getting organized sounds so complicated— and, frankly, *boring*—that it hardly seems worthwhile.

This book will show you how to do it—and how it can be both simple and interesting. It gives you GO (Get-Organized) techniques: a handful or two of keywords that are easy to remember and simple to apply; a system so basic that you can use it to pack a suitcase, clean your room, or get the job you want.

In short, the GO system will enable you to GO for it, whatever "it" may be; it's first aid that will get you going.

Your life could probably use some first aid. It's a good bet that you've got too much to do, too much to think about, too much to worry about, including:

family, school, job, friends
social life, love life, inner life
demands, responsibilities, opportunities, decisions
people, places, things, ideas, situations
homework, housework, sports, clubs
today, tomorrow, next week, next year, graduation
what to do, what to be, how to get there

First aid? Crutches and a transplant are more like it! And that's when things are going smoothly. When a *problem* intrudes into your thirty-six-hour day, well . . .

Sometimes, don't you just want to stay in bed and pull the covers over your head? Forever? It's all just too much.

With this book and its simple organizing system that you can put into practice as soon as you start reading about it, you can take that "too much" and make the most of it.

So get organized; it's not hard. In fact, you'll learn in the next chapter that the best way to go about it is to . . .

- "Take It Easy." Here you'll find the three simple principles you need to remember to put your life or any part of it in order. Do they work? Yes—and you can prove that to yourself even before you've finished the chapter.
- "Get Set." In Chapter Two, you'll learn how to apply these principles to three practical strategies that will help you to decide on your goals and how to reach them. Then see for yourself that they work.
- "Act." Chapter Three introduces three techniques for forming an action plan toward success in any activity.

In short, GO is a nine-byte memory's worth of organizational tips set out in a simple format that is designed to occupy the least possible space in your busy brain. And it is flexible enough to fit *your* needs for organizing *your* time and activities in a way that will let you succeed at all you must do—and still have time for all you want to do.

Getting organized doesn't take long, it's not boring, and it *does* work. Besides, it's easy. How easy? Turn the page and see.

ONE

TAKE IT EASY

The Three Principles of Good Organization:

Simplicity—Order—Steps

Jessie is just waking up, and already her mind is buzzing with the day she faces:

She has to get up, get washed and dressed, and catch her ride to school, where, in second period, she has a quiz. Second period—that's before history, and next week in history there's a big exam. . . . Before she goes to school she has to call two of her friends about where to meet for lunch. And, oh yes, she has to take lunch because she's starting her diet today for sure, and, anyway, she's spent her allowance for the week even though it's only . . . what? Tuesday? Tuesday.

Tuesday—oh no! basketball tryouts. But then when will she go to the library to finish research for the paper due on Friday? And Friday there's that party—but, oh my gosh, she's supposed to go visit her dad this weekend. How can she do both, and what will she take to wear? There's that cute guy in her dad's building—cuter than Gary—and Gary's birthday is . . . when? Sunday?

Sunday—oh lordy, she's got to get him a present. She's really going to have to find a job. There's just not enough money, especially if she wants to take a trip this summer . . . but she needs to work this summer, too! The Hoovers asked her to baby-sit this Thursday night—that's good. But then when will she finish writing the paper? And now her mother is calling, reminding Jessie that it's her day to walk Nathan to school because it's Mom's early workday. "And Jessie—don't forget the groceries. The list is on the fridge!"

All Jessie wants to do is dive back under the covers. But she doesn't because she has to get dressed—fast! One look around her room and she groans. How will she ever find her blue skirt in this mess?

She races around anyway, throwing clothes this way and that—locating her skirt and losing her notebook—until, by the time she's half-dressed, she's forgotten what she's supposed to do next.

Jessie's day may sound familiar to you—different only in detail from a day in your own life. It hasn't really started yet, but she's already in a panic of activity—so much activity that it's unlikely she'll accomplish anything.

Or are you more like Jake?

He woke up facing a day not unlike Jessie's except that he has two quizzes today—but he's not worried about that. What's on Jake's mind as he lies in bed tightening the knot in his stomach are some BIG questions.

Like . . . what if he doesn't get an A in chemistry? Then he won't get into honors physics and for sure he won't get into the college he wants to. But where does he want to go to school? And which colleges will accept him? If only they'd give the exams now he'd do all right. He wishes he weren't only in the tenth grade so that this would be all over. Or does he want to go to college at all? But he has to. He really wants a career . . . no nickel-and-dime stuff! Of course, what he'd really like to do is play professional sports, or at least be a coach. He could make the track team with no sweat— he's a good runner—but he likes baseball better, even if he's not that good. If only he had practiced more last year he'd be on the JV ball team now and he'd have half a chance. But how could he practice? His parents didn't give him a big enough allowance, so he had to take a paper route and was always too tired and busy to practice. Darn! How much money had he saved up from that? Thirty-five dollars.

What he needs is more money—that's what he needs—because what if he can't get a scholarship? If only he had a car, he could get a good job, delivering pizzas. Of course he won't be old enough to get a license for almost a year. How much money can he save by then so he can get a car? Oh no—it's impossible! Would Dad let him use the car? No—not him! Dad never let Jake do anything. If only he had different parents and they were really rich. Then he wouldn't have to worry about anything and he could go to college anywhere he wanted. But where did he want to go to college? Would they take him, with his average?

By now Jake is so tightly wrapped up in his own thoughts that he doesn't hear his mother call him, and he finally gets up so late he has to go to school with no breakfast and gets only a 79 on his first quiz.

Jake is so firmly focused on the big issues in his past and future—most of which he can, in fact, do nothing about— that he's paralyzed and can't cope with *today*. Does that sound familiar?

Jake and Jessie need some first aid if they're to get organized and GO for what they want out of their days, their weeks, and their futures. Like many crisis victims, they are resisting rescue by either freezing into dangerous paralysis or erupting into self-defeating panic. Jake is paralyzed by what he perceives as his problems, and Jessie's panic will prevent her from managing half of what she thinks she has to manage.

What they really need to do—what *you* need to do—is to *Take It Easy*. Begin by taking a deep breath, because . . .

You're about to take your life in your hands. That probably seems overwhelming—in fact, that's why getting organized can seem complicated: There's just *too much*.

Your life is, indeed, too big to look at—so look at your hand.

How many fingers do you see?

You'll only need three of them to get into the GO system for getting organized.

Finger by finger, count off the system's three *principles:*

1. Simplicity
2. Order
3. Steps

Just remember S–O–S—a "first-aid kit"—whenever rescue is needed.

Simplicity–Order–Steps may sound not only simple, but simple*minded*. Don't be fooled, though: The system works, as you'll agree by the time you finish reading this chapter. Besides, you've got a complicated life, so why not simplify it? The principles described here will help you do that. So start right now, with:

PRINCIPLE 1. SIMPLICITY

"Simple" is *the* key word for this system. We might almost say that this book is not so much about how to get organized as it is about how to *simplify*.

"What's all this talk about 'simplicity'? That might work for *other* people, but *my* life is complicated!"

If that sounds like you—stop. Remember that the most complex computer program is built on only two basic commands: ON/1 and OFF/0. So take another deep breath, and just memorize this phrase: "If it's not simple, something's wrong."

Jessie's day seems very complicated. Just getting *dressed* is complicated because she can't find her clothes. Finding her blue skirt takes time away from the other things she wants to do. She might get through her day, but even if she gets most of the things done she wants to, chances are she won't enjoy much of it. Just as she ought to sort out her closet (or at least her floor), she ought to sort out her day ahead of time so that she can do and enjoy the things she really wants to and has to do.

Jake's day won't be simple, either, because his life isn't simple. His life isn't simple because he's *making* it complicated. He's dragging through this one day such a load from the past and future that he can't focus on or enjoy what's happening now. He'd do better if he would remember the phrase that started this section and say it again (and again and again): "If it's not simple, something's wrong."

To simplify means "to reduce to basic essentials." If, when confronted by an impossibly baffling situation, you look for the *simplest* solution, you'll have it made.

Simpleminded? Obviously not geared to *your* complicated life-style?

Well, consider this: Scientists *love* simple solutions; they call them "elegant." And when tackling a problem of cosmic proportions, the most sophisticated scientist asks, "What is the simplest solution?"

Professional engineers even have a word for it: KISS, which stands for "*Keep It Simple, Stupid!*" They know that a bridge with a complex design, for instance, not only costs more but is more likely to fall down than is a bridge with a simple design.

You see, being "smart" is so important that most of us get *too* smart for our own good, at least occasionally. Jessie has gotten so "smart" about juggling all the events of her day—usually at the last minute—that she can't see how it works against her. And, like her, most of us are so "smart" that we complicate even the most basic tasks, the most obvious situations. Jessie would have a better day if, instead of juggling everything she has to do, she'd spend a few minutes simplifying. How? Like this:

Take a Look

The first simple step to take in organizing a messy situation is to *take a look* at it—take a step back from it and get the whole picture. If you're doing a jigsaw puzzle, for example, you can make it easier if you look at the picture on the box first. If you're writing a term paper, you'll do better if you decide what you're going to write about before you start your research. Jessie will be less likely to snack on candy if she has a clear overview of her diet plan.

If we act moment by moment, reacting to each situation separately, when we run up against a truly complex problem or a jam-packed day, things will really get out of hand because we will be adding confusion to the tasks we must accomplish.

By taking a look ahead and absorbing as much information as possible, we can answer the question, "What is the *simplest* solution?"

Take Apart

To simplify, to "reduce to basic essentials," means to break big things—problems, projects, situations, issues—down into their smallest parts. If you're doing a jigsaw puzzle, you'll enjoy it more if you take the pieces apart before you put them together. When you're assigned a topic for a term paper, you know you're not supposed to write about everything you can find on that topic. You have to narrow the topic—break it down—and then break it down further into sections and ideas. Then you write the term paper, not in one massive burst of words, but one paragraph, one sentence at a time. Jake needs to see that doing well on today's quizzes *is* a part of getting into college.

One simple way to *take apart* any complicated situation is to answer a series of simple questions:

> *Must* it be done?
> Must it be done *now?*
> Must it be done now *by me?*

The answers to them can help you *take away* what's not necessary.

Take Away

Keeping it simple means dealing only with what's in front of you. If Jake took some of the mental energy and attention he devotes to the past and the future and put them into his tasks today, not only would each of his days be better organized and more manageable, but the days would add up and the future would happen without much effort on his part.

We complicate things when we're distracted by past, future, or side issues. Clearing away the "what ifs" and "if onlies" helps you to get to the "I cans": "If only" Jake hadn't had to take a paper route . . . So what? "What if" he doesn't get into the college he wants? Can he do anything about that *now?* He can't change the past. He can't predict the future. What *can* he do? He can make the most of today.

Think of it this way: When you're eating supper, are you thinking about what's for breakfast? Or are you focusing on what's on your plate now—deciding what to eat first, what you'll leave, and what you want seconds on? You'll have a more satisfying meal if you deal only with what's in front of you *now*.

Or when you're at bat, are you thinking about the postgame party? You won't get a hit. If, when you drive, your mind or your eyes are focused five miles down the road, you're in deep trouble.

Of course, no single activity exists by itself. When you munch on your dinner pork chop, you're engaged in the larger process of fueling yourself; when you step to the plate, that's part of an overall effort to win the game. If Jake weren't looking ahead to college, he wouldn't care so much about his activities today.

The point, however, is that the only sensible way to manage these larger issues, processes, and goals is to deal with the task or project at hand.

And what if you *can't* do what's in front of you? You can take away that "impossibility" by simply *asking for help*. Jake can find out how to get into college and how to get financial aid by turning to the experts who can take him through the process. By taking this simple step toward his future, he will give himself some peace of mind and the energy to GO for the *important* things in his present. That's S–O–S in its most basic meaning. Often the simplest solution to any "impossible" situation is to say "HELP!" so that you can move on from "what's now" to "what's next."

Take Another Look

How do we decide what's important? If there's too much to do, simplify; for each "to do," ask "why?" or "who says?"

Why does Jessie have to start her diet today? *Who says* she should be the one to organize lunch? If it's just too much, maybe these are things she can take away today.

How's this for simple? "If it ain't broke, don't fix it!" Jake may not be able to make the baseball team, but he's good at running track. So what's his problem? His athletic life isn't so "broke" that it needs fixing. So why complicate things by trying to turn himself into a ball player?

Once we've reduced our days and weeks to the essentials, what's the simplest way to get through them smoothly?

Put them in some kind of sensible *order*.

PRINCIPLE 2. ORDER

The best way to put anything in order—to sort it out, to prepare to plan and take action on it—is (you guessed it) the *simplest* way. And the simplest way to put anything—a day, a puzzle, or a closet—in order is to do:

First Things First

That sounds pretty obvious, doesn't it? When you have more than one thing to do, do the first thing first.

If Jessie were doing first things first, she'd wash and dress before she started juggling her week. And Jake, instead of lying around brooding over the faraway past and future, would be studying for his quizzes.

"Of course," you say. Well, how about you?

If you're like most people, you violate the silly-sounding principle of doing first things first—and suffer the consequences—on a regular basis.

For instance, how many times lately have you . . .

spent hours on the phone or in front of the television set when you had an exam the next day?

sworn to lose ten pounds and not been able to resist
a candy bar after school?
made a date to go to the movies on Friday and then
spent your allowance by Thursday?
planned the clothes you wanted to wear and then
forgotten to check the dirty-laundry bag?

First things first means

doing *A* and *B* before you get to *C*.
taking care of the most urgent business first.
working hardest toward the most important goals.

Of course, all of that takes knowing which is *A,* what is
most urgent, and what is most important.

Keeping the principle of simplicity in mind, the simplest
way to decide what comes first is to ask, "What must be
done *now?*"

First, Now

Ordering your time by the simple first-things-first principle
means focusing on the most immediate tasks first and ignoring the most distant tasks. In other words, what must be
done *now?*

For Jake, it's obviously important that he get into college—
but he can't take care of that *today.* Instead, he should be
concerned with his quizzes; they come first.

And what about you? If you want to give a successful party,
you'll invite your friends well in advance and buy the food
and drink right before the party. Otherwise, you're likely to
end up with a lot of snacks in an empty room.

Now comes first in terms of the *sequence* of tasks, too.
Jessie's day is, to say the least, going to be full. But before
she begins it, she has to get dressed—which is not going to

be easy, given the state of her clothes. Does that mean she should stop everything and clean her closet? Not *now!* Sure— if she'd taken some time over the weekend to get her clothing organized, or if she had even done it the night before, she'd have one less activity to factor into today's sequence. But for now, she should shake out the neatest blue skirt and top and just get going.

Doing things in sequence is often not only convenient, but critical. At the grocery store, for instance, it's a waste of time and money to put the ice cream in the cart first. A cake or a chemistry experiment simply won't be any good if you don't follow the sequence printed on the box or in the book. You need to research the paper *before* you write it.

First Choices

First also means "most important." Which is more important to Jessie: the party on Friday or her scheduled visit with her dad? Only she can decide, just as only Jake can decide whether it's more important to have spending money or to save up for a car.

Which would be more important to you? A diet or a candy bar? The phone call or the exam? It depends on what you value more: losing weight over time or satisfying your hunger now; keeping a good friend or getting a good grade. If playing professional baseball were really an important goal of Jake's, he probably could have found a way to play ball somewhere.

Which of the activities on your own agenda you place first should depend on what *you* consider most important. Others would place different "to dos" at the top of their lists.

You probably have some idea of what's important in *your* life, and a little later in the book you'll have a chance to get clearer about which goals you value most. However grand or fuzzy those goals seem now, you'll be able to work toward them in a simple, orderly fashion if you do it step by step.

PRINCIPLE 3. STEPS

No matter how busy Jessie's brain is this morning, she can't get through her whole day or week at once; and Jake, despite the way his mind is working, can't get through his whole *life* today. They are feeling overwhelmed because they're trying to deal with everything at once.

They, like anyone else, can only do one thing at a time. For instance:

When you're ready to apply to college, will you send applications to every school in the country and then decide? To find a job, will you answer every ad in the Sunday classifieds and then sort through the responses you get?

When the doctor prescribes medicine to cure an infection, you can't get well faster by taking all the pills at once. If you want to lose fifteen pounds, you won't have much long-term success if you try to do it in three days of fasting and jogging. You may have already learned, to your regret, that if you decide to devote only the last week of the semester to researching and writing all of your term papers, you're in trouble. You might get it done, but the exhaustion! And the grades?

You get the point: You could manage any of these projects with a lot more success (and have a lot more time for fun) if you would tackle the steps they require one at a time.

Simple Steps

Step by step is the *simple* way to success.

We may all wish to be superhuman, but the fact is, we can do only one thing at a time. No matter how mindboggling a computer's operations seem, the computer in fact performs only one operation at a time.

The closet needs cleaning, the bike needs fixing, and you've promised to make cookies for the bake sale. So you take everything out of the closet, dismantle the bike, and spread the cookie ingredients on top of the counter, right? Not if you want to tackle these projects in the simplest way.

To simplify, we reduce to the basic essentials; so to simplify an activity, we break it into steps. The simplest way to succeed at any of these projects is to take the steps that each requires one at a time.

Embarking on all your projects at once—whether baking cookies or losing fifteen pounds—may *seem* to save time, but does it work? No!

Orderly Steps

Step by step is also the *orderly* way.

If you were going to put together a model airplane, would you paint all the little pieces first?

Or to bake a cake, do you beat the flour and sugar well, then dump in the eggs after you've placed the pans in the oven?

And what happens if you read the instructions for an exam *after* you've answered all the questions? Disaster!

Success comes from breaking a project down into its steps and then taking the first step first.

Taking one step at a time may sound boring to you, or you may be the kind of person who avoids tackling a project because of all the steps it will take.

The good news about steps is that *anyone* can do *anything* step by step.

Jessie's pals, Marilyn and Marvin, provide an example.

Marilyn is a bundle of energy: She has an imagination that knows no bounds when it comes to dreaming up projects, and she's always the first to volunteer to help anyone do any-

thing. Not only that, but when she gets an assignment or an idea, she absolutely has to do it right this minute or she won't be able to sleep tonight.

She's always been like that. Her mother says that even when she was an infant, she never napped for more than twenty minutes, and now she's the busiest teenager in the neighborhood and she doesn't take naps at all. In fact, she's always tired— and she often feels that she could have done something better if she hadn't rushed through it in order to make the next event.

Practicing the step-by-step approach can help a "doer" like Marilyn. She might, for instance, make a list of reasonable goals for a given day and then rest serenely at night, gathering her energy for the next day's activities.

Marvin, on the other hand, is called "laid back" by some, "lazy" by others. Marvin's motto is, "There is nothing so important that it can't be put off until tomorrow." He's not really lazy; he—well, we don't need to go into his psychology. The point is, he's the opposite of Marilyn, who has to do everything today. Marvin is a procrastinator. That long word comes from a few short Latin words which mean, literally, "putting off until tomorrow."

The step-by-step approach will help Marvin, too, because the bulk of the things he ought to be doing *can* be put off until tomorrow. To succeed in even the most laid-back way, all he has to do today is to take one step on any project.

Now or Later?

Which one of these people do you identify with? Are you a "doer" like Marilyn or a procrastinator like Marvin?

If you're not sure, stop now and do a quick self-survey because it will make a difference when you begin to put the GO system into practice.

Answer these questions in your own mind:

1. In class, I usually
   - *A.* am first to raise my hand.
   - *B.* wait until I'm called on.
2. I am more comfortable
   - *A.* doing the task at hand without thinking about the future.
   - *B.* thinking about my future and letting today take care of itself.
3. I like to
   - *A.* start on a project as soon as it's assigned or as soon as I think of it.
   - *B.* attack a project at the last minute because I work well under pressure.
4. I
   - *A.* seldom
   - *B.* usually
   get enough rest.
5. If I ignore a problem long enough, it will
   - *A.* get worse.
   - *B.* go away.
6. Among my friends, I am the one who usually
   - *A.* gets things going.
   - *B.* goes along with the gang.
7. People usually
   - *A.* expect too much of me. I feel overwhelmed.
   - *B.* don't ask me to do much. I feel left out.
8. In my free time, I like to
   - *A.* keep busy.
   - *B.* relax.

   A answers indicate a doer; *B* answers indicate a procrastinator.

If you feel *very* strongly about your responses, whether *A* or *B*, you may be a perfectionist. An *over*doer like Marilyn keeps overbusy because she's afraid that she'll be considered a "failure" if she doesn't do everything and do it right. Someone who is paralyzed by procrastination, as Marvin often is, may be afraid to do anything because of the same fear of failure.

Whatever type you are, and whatever the reason, you can be a success if you take things step by step because taking things in steps means: "Take it *easy*, but take it."

That means that you don't have to do it all at once but you do have to do *something*. So if you're feeling overwhelmed by "too much to do" or paralyzed by "I can't do anything," remember the basic GO motto—"If it's not simple, something's wrong"—and try tackling your tasks in the simple, orderly way, *step by step*.

How do you go about that? In *order*. And order begins with first things first.

This all sounds simple, but will it work? Let's try S–O–S on those sinking "ships," Jake and Jessie.

Jessie has made her day—her whole week, in fact—so complicated that she's not going to be able to do everything she *has* to do, much less most of what she *wants* to do. She needs S–O–S—Simplicity, Order, and Steps.

When she takes a look at her day, she sees these "parts":

   clothes
   schoolwork
   after-school activities
   friends
   money
   family

Think about S–O–S in terms of her clothes, for instance. She may not yet be so organized that all the clean ones are hanging neatly or folded in her drawers and the dirty ones are in the laundry hamper. But she can save herself a lot of time and frazzle if, when she's undressing on Monday night, she gives some thought to tomorrow's outfit. What did the radio announcer say about the weather? And if she has basketball tryouts, does she have something simple to get in and out of?

All she has to do then is drape the skirt and top over a chair or the doorknob where they're easy to see and she will have one less thing to think about on Tuesday morning.

The same think-ahead approach will help her get the other pieces of her day and week set for action. None of her upcoming activities is a surprise, so what happens if she takes a few minutes on Sunday to sort out the upcoming week and, while she's lying in bed Monday night, give some thought to Tuesday?

What happens? Here's what happens—with a little S–O–S:

Jessie has set her alarm fifteen minutes early because Tuesday's her day to take Nathan to school, and, since she's starting her diet today, she has to make a salad for herself for lunch. Besides, her diet will work better if she gives herself time to walk. She's talked her friends into having a picnic lunch because if she spends too much money on food, she won't be able to buy Gary a present. She's planning to get him something at the shopping center when she goes for groceries. If she gets it now, she'll know how much money she has left over for the week—maybe enough to buy something new for the party or to wear to Dad's in case she meets that cute guy (that is, if she takes her lunch a few more days this week).

Besides, if she gives Gary the present early, he'll be more willing to give her a ride from Friday's party to her dad's place. (Boy! Was Dad mad when she said she might not see him till Saturday!)

While she's eating breakfast, she takes a quick glance at her notes for the second-period quiz. She's hoping there won't be too much homework today because, if there isn't, she can get at least some of it done while she's waiting her turn at the basketball tryouts, and later she might have time to get started on that paper.

Wait—an idea! If she gets some kind of quickie fixings at the grocery store and makes supper, her mother will probably be willing to drive her to the library so she can get the books she needs. That way, she can get at the research and finish up when she's sitting at the Hoovers'. They seem to want her as a regular sitter, so she'll try to work out a good deal with them—then she'll be able to count on some extra cash.

But in the meantime, there's a terrific movie on TV tonight— and if things go as she plans, she'll have time to enjoy it!

Now Jessie has a simple, orderly day that she's gone through step by step with less panic and more fun than she would have had otherwise. To make her day work, Jessie had to do some thinking ahead. Is it worth the trouble? Well— look what it can get Jessie: time, money, and success. And in the process, it will help her feel more comfortable with herself and her family. Not bad!

Jake, on the other hand, thinks ahead *too* much—and with little good result. He has lots of goals, dreams, and wishes, but he needs to focus on what he can do *today* toward achieving them. A few GO principles will help him worry less about— and make more of—all the issues in his life: school, money, family, and his own feelings about himself. Here's how:

Jake wakes up and stretches, then remembers his new promise to himself. For the second day in a row he does some aerobics and lifts weights. (He's decided to try out for the cross-country team.) The coach says he has the body for it, if he could just build up a little strength and stamina. In fact, he might have time to jog to school if he gets going, so he takes only a glance at the Ivy League catalogs on his shelf and at the used-car ads he's tacked to the bulletin board (with the prices circled).

While eating breakfast, he reviews his notes for the quizzes today—no problem! He's glad that studying has never been hard for him because he'll have less time for it now that he's decided to get an after-school and weekend job. This afternoon, he's going to the sporting goods store—that's where he'd really like to work because they give employee discounts. The first thing he wants is a basketball, if the price is right, because his is shot and he wants to get some of the guys together for a regular game.

Jake is going to have a good day. He's simplified his life by ignoring some of the "what ifs" and "if onlies." Instead of trying to fix what isn't broken, he's making the most of who he is and what he can do. He hasn't given up on his goals, but he's working toward them in order and step by step.

Besides—he's feeling pretty good about himself, and there's not even one knot in his stomach.

So, is getting organized the S–O–S way worth it? It works for Jake and Jessie—and it can work for you, once you've had a little practice.

Try it!

TRY IT!

Getting into the habit of getting organized with the S–O–S principles takes what every new skill takes: *practice*. That's what this section—and *all* of the book's "Try It!" sections— are for. Make full use of them to get in gear to GO.

First, a tip. When you read through the examples that follow, they may seem, at first, to make ordinary tasks more complicated rather than simpler. But that's probably what your first driving lesson, basketball workout, computer manual, or dance class seemed to do in the beginning. Yet with a little practice, those skills became so automatic that it's hard to remember you ever had to learn them. The same is true for the S–O–S system.

You'll also find that the specific principles outlined here apply to *any* task or goal you have.

So read through the examples once, and then again. As you read through them the second time, do this:

1. Compare the techniques described here with those that you usually use—and think about how the results from your system compare with the ones you'd get from this one.
2. Think about other familiar activities you could apply S–O–S to—for instance, packing a suitcase. How do you pack a suitcase? Do you fold up as much stuff as will fit and squeeze the suitcase shut? That technique may be the quickest one, the one that solves the problem for the moment. But the result is that your trip is more about coping with wrinkled clothes, not enough underwear, too few shirts, and no extra jeans than about enjoying the experience of travel.

To pack a suitcase, think S–O–S!

Simplicity

First, *take a look:* How long is the trip? What will the weather be where you're going? What activities do you plan? What are the customs or fashions there? How much can you carry? When must you be ready to go?

Second, *take apart:* What do you have? What must you buy? What must you clean? Make a list. Then find someplace to lay out *everything* you want to take.

Third, *take away:* Eliminate what you really don't need and what won't fit in the suitcase. Check your list after reviewing step 1. Mix and match clothing in order to pare the list down to the minimum needed to keep you comfortable.

Fourth, *take another look:* Test to see if what remains on the list will fit in the luggage. If it doesn't, do steps 1, 2, and 3 again.

Order

First, *first things first:* Know where you're going before you plan. Plan before you pack. Plan before you shop or wash the things you plan to pack. Pack before you leave!

Second, *first, now:* What must be done when? Know your deadlines. Give yourself enough time for sensible choices, but don't pack too soon or everything will get scrunched.

Third, *first choices:* Choose what's most important. Leave out the rest unless you have some extra room.

Steps

First, *simple steps:* Put everything you want to pack within easy reach at a time when you can focus on the project. Check your list again.

Second, *orderly steps:* Piece by piece, place the biggest, heaviest items so they'll end up on the bottom of the bag, and the lightest, most delicate ones where they'll be best protected. Put little things into big ones. Think ahead: What will you want to take out first? Keep that handy. Group similar items—put your socks inside your shoes, your soap with your washcloth—to make life easier when you unpack.

Now, try to close the suitcase. If it won't close, *simplify.* Take another look, take apart again, and take away some more!

With this S–O–S suitcase, you're really ready to get up and GO for a trip. Without having to think about such things as wardrobe and toothpaste, you can take it easy and feel free to get the most out of your travel.

That's the point of getting organized for anything: to gain ease and freedom. And what works for packing a suitcase works for any other activity. For instance, when you are **studying for an exam,** you'll be better prepared if you approach it the same way we packed that suitcase.

Simplicity

Take a look at what you have to study for—and *only* for—that exam. Take apart the material—chapter by chapter, or notes, readings, outline. Take away everything that's not needed for that test—as well as any activities or homework that you don't have to do right now.

Order

Think "first things first," and arrange your time so that you have enough of it, with a little left over for a quick review right before the test. Organize your task by "first things first," too: Memorize, analyze, or practice the most important topics first—the big issues or the formulas the teacher has stressed. The little stuff that fits into this mental outline will then be easier to remember.

Steps

Once you've gotten an idea of what needs doing, go through the material one piece at a time, ending each study session with a quick review.

Will S–O–S work for something as complicated as **cooking dinner**? Watch!

First, simplify by taking a look at what it will take:

Your mom is working late, and dinner has to be on the table by 7 o'clock so that your sister can get to her baby-sitting job. On the menu: roast chicken, fresh broccoli, and brown rice. It's now 5:30. The chicken will take an hour and 15 minutes to bake. The broccoli takes 8 minutes in the microwave; the rice takes 25 minutes on the top of the stove. There's a dessert mix on the shelf that has to chill an hour in the fridge. You'll need to empty the dishwasher and set the table. Oh—there's no milk. And when will you get to your homework?

Will you have time for all this in an hour and a half? Don't get out a calculator. Instead, just put the time and tasks in order. Try it!

You can get all the noncooking done—from going for milk to setting the table—before you start cooking. But that way, dinner will never be ready in time.

Instead, you can use the simple, orderly, step-by-step process. You can turn on the oven, get the chicken ready in the pan, and start it baking. Then you can mix up the dessert and put it in the fridge. Once this is in process, you'll have time for all the other steps, including some of your homework— especially if you send your brother out for the milk.

From these examples, you should be getting the idea that the S–O–S principles *can* get you going. And the principles can be applied to any number of projects, including:

> giving a party
> studying for an exam
> writing a paper
> cleaning a room
> finding a job
> applying to college
> planning a day
> organizing a week at school, work, or play
> plotting a year—with an eye to the future
> organizing an event
> taking a trip
> shopping

building a loft bed
repairing a car or bike
starting a diet or an exercise program

How? By counting off on your fingertips the simple, orderly steps you need to GO for it.

1. Simplicity: Take a look, take apart, take away. In other words, *simplify*.
2. Order: Think "first things first" when arranging time and projects.
3. Steps: Succeed by taking one step at a time, in order.

You've got it! Your S–O–S "first-aid kit": an all-purpose system for getting organized—one that begins with the idea that "if it's not simple, something's wrong" and ends with the rule "take it easy, but take it."

How hard could this be? Not very! So go to the next chapter, and get set to put it to work.

T W O

GET SET

The Three Strategies of Good Organization:

Aim—Countdown—Takeoff

Think of the S–O–S principles—Simplicity, Order, Steps— as the same kind of first-aid kit that you might put into your glove compartment, suitcase, or backpack before you set off on a trip. Just as that kit helps you to cope with the emergencies that can keep you from enjoying your trip, S–O–S helps you to deal productively with the demands of your day and the issues of your life.

Here's how:

Imagine that you're about to take a trip by car to someplace you've never been before.

You know generally how to read a map: You've learned in school how to interpret the commonly used symbols so that, when you look at a map, you can figure out how to make sense of it. In the same way, you've learned the S–O–S basics of the GO system and you can count them off on three fingers: Simplicity, Order, Steps.

These principles show you how to "get ready." Now, just as easily, you can "get set."

Before you take off on that car trip, you need to put your map-reading skills to *practical* use. To plan a trip, you need to know:

> where you're going.
> when you want to leave and arrive.
> how best to get there.

In the same way, to get set for success in any project, you need good organization. That means to:

> set your goals—Aim for where to go.
> set the clock—Count down for when to go.
> set your course—for Takeoff on how to get there.

The initials for Aim, Countdown, and Takeoff spell A–C–T, which can serve as another way to help remember, if you need to, the next steps in the GO process.

You can count off A–C–T on the fingers of your other hand and put them together with the S–O–S fingers to remember that just as a rescue vessel gets a sinking ship back on course, "S–O–S helps you A–C–T."

In this chapter, you'll learn *strategies* for applying S–O–S to take Aim and determine your personal destination, Count down from your deadlines and figure out your GO-for-it timetable, and plan the Takeoff that will head you in the direction that suits *you* best.

So get your pad of paper and a pencil (with an eraser) now, because you'll need them as you start to put S–O–S to work for you.

STRATEGY 1. AIM

"I'd like to take a trip."

Will that desire get you very far? Not likely—not yet, anyway. It *sounds* simple enough, but . . .

Where? is the first question you must answer before setting off on either a long journey or a short errand. If you don't know where you're going, how are you to get there? That may be so obvious as to sound silly, but without direction, we just wander—and it is only the rare few who have the funds and freedom to take trips to nowhere.

The same applies to getting organized, yet a surprising number of people think more about *how* to get something done than about the end result of it. To GO for it successfully, you have to know what "it" is.

According to the dictionary, a *goal* is "the end toward which effort is directed." It can be something to be, to buy, to win, or to become—today or someday. But if you're going to organize your efforts, you need a goal of some kind—whether it's packing a suitcase or becoming a doctor.

We tend to think of goals as something grand, something to aim high for—but goals can also be simple, everyday objectives. Getting dressed is a daily goal, for instance. There's not much we can achieve without reaching that goal first.

You should take the same approach to planning a day or a party as you take to applying to college or charting a career, feeding the hungry or finding a cure for cancer. You should take simple, orderly steps.

Goals Get You Going

Goals—whether lifelong dreams or a day's worth of chores—make good organization possible.

How so? The explanation is as easy as S–O–S.

Aiming toward goals Simplifies life. If Jake sets a goal of earning a certain amount of money each week, getting a car becomes simpler. A travel agent will have a much easier time helping you make arrangements if you have a specific destination in mind than if you say, "I want to go somewhere."

Goals bring Order. Jake will have a much more orderly day if he focuses on today's goals rather than on those years ahead. The more detailed the goal, the more order it brings.

Goals help us to succeed by Steps. The more Jake focuses on the steps that will lead to his ultimate goal of college or a car, the more likely he is to reach it.

Not only do goals make good organization possible, but the reverse is also true: Good organization can help you achieve even the most "impossible" of goals.

What are Jessie's chances of finding a good-paying job that she can fit into her schedule? Not bad—if she stops wishing and sets to work toward a specific goal. If you've got the urge to travel around the world, you can satisfy it by turning that urge into an attainable goal.

What are some of *your* goals? What do you dream of? Where would you like to be in four years? What do you want to do next week? What must be done today? Take your pad of paper and jot down your answers—as many as possible and as fast as possible. Then set the list aside.

The lists that Jessie and Jake make might look like this:

Jessie

have more money	lose weight
look better	have friends like me
more time	be a better person
do well in school	new clothes
boyfriends	get a job
basketball team	trip this summer
deal better with family	

Jake

good college	better body
car	be happy
cross-country team	better grades
money	big career

Some people may think that they don't want goals, that they like to "take life as it comes." Or they may not be aware that they have goals. If either of these sounds like you, take a look at this list of the major areas (not necessarily in order of importance) of your life:

school
family
money
friends
appearance
free-time activities
personal achievement

Now try to write down at least one goal in each area.

Once you start, you'll probably think of a lot more—and that's good. Because living without goals, "taking life as it comes," does not necessarily make for a laid-back and easygoing life. Quite the opposite, in fact. A person who isn't going for anything is going for everything, tied to a pattern of *reaction* to random events rather than to the freedom of taking *action*. Much as we may wish it weren't true, we all have things we *must* do. And getting those "musts" organized with some of our personal goals in mind results in more time for what we *want* to do. With goals, we can take selective action—doing what needs to be done, yes, but doing *only* what needs to be done.

Or you may feel that there are so many goals you can't possibly attain any of them, let alone write them down. Then start applying S–O–S first aid.

When Jessie and Jake take a look at their lists, they see a lot of important goals—and so do you, now that you've thought about it. How can they—and you—possibly accomplish these goals and still have time for homework? By *simplifying*.

And the first step toward simplicity is to take apart big goals into smaller pieces.

W–H–O Says?

To break goals down, how about dividing them into "possible" goals and "impossible" goals? No such thing!

How about into "good" or "right" and "bad" or "wrong" goals? Well . . .

On Jake's and Jessie's lists, are any goals "right" or "wrong"? Of course none of them is wrong—because each of them is right for the person who has set them.

This is the same as when people plan trips: They don't all head for the same place. They travel toward their own destinations.

And are all those travelers journeying because they *want* to? No. Some are on pleasure trips, but others are traveling for business or to meet some other kind of responsibility.

When traveling, you pick a destination because it is someplace where you:

> *want* to go, like an amusement park, for vacation.
> *have* to go, like back to school.
> *ought* to go, like to your elderly Aunt Martha's.

Jake *wants* a car. . . . Jessie *has* to get her school paper done. . . . Jake *ought* to study for his quizzes. Or how about this series of goals that you may work toward without even realizing it:

You *want* to graduate, so . . .
you *have* to go to school; and since it's cold out . . .
you *ought* to dress warmly.

You'll have a better idea of how to GO for your major and minor goals when you break them down into these three categories:

want to . . .
have to . . .
ought to . . .

When Jessie writes Want to, Have to, and Ought to (or their initials, W–H–O) across the top of a sheet of paper, she can sort her list of goals into the appropriate columns.

This will become her "GO-for-it" chart. Like the itinerary for a trip, it will be a reminder of where she's going. You'll be making your own GO chart soon, so start thinking about it as you follow Jessie's chart.

W (want to)	*H* (have to)	*O* (ought to)
look better	have more	help Mom
boyfriends	money	lose weight
basketball	do well in	talk more with
team	school	Dad
more friends	more time	be a better
summer trip	get a job	person

Writing out her goals like this makes it easy for Jessie to see what she's aiming for—and to see that she's got a *lot* to aim for.

To further simplify, she can find a way to focus on the goals that mean the most in each of her W–H–O columns. And she can do that by asking, for each item on her chart, "W–H–O says?" That way, she begins to put her goals in the order of "first things first," or, Which is more important?

"W–H–O says?" is another way of asking, Why? And it's an important way of asking that question because often the goals that we aim for are ones that are set, not by us, but by someone else.

A goal for a business traveler or for someone on an emergency mission is "to get there as fast as possible." But that's *not* an important goal for the tourist who wants to see the countryside.

Which is likely to be more important to Jake in the long run: getting on the cross-country team or getting good grades?

Which would you guess is more important to Jessie—"be a better person" or "talk more with Dad"?

Let's see, she's numbered the goals in each column in order of their importance.

W	*H*	*O*
3 look better	1 have more money	2 help Mom
2 boyfriends	3 do well in school	3 lose weight
4 basketball team	2 more time	4 talk more with Dad
1 more friends	4 get a job	1 be a better person
5 summer trip		

Who says those are her most important goals? She does. Would they be the same as yours? Probably not. The relative importance *you* attach to each of your goals comes out of your own values.

Values? How did values get into this? You only wanted to get organized! Well, since a value is something you prize, esteem, or consider worthy, it's obvious that you'll rank your goals according to your values.

But don't worry—you needn't know your values to put your goals in order. In fact, the order of importance in which you place your goals will show a lot about your values.

From Jessie's chart, it looks as though she values highly

getting along well with people, including herself.

But has she gotten any closer to *achieving* her goals? Not really. In fact, some of her goals—such as "get a job" and "have more time"—even conflict with one another. How can she reach one without missing the other?

Isn't this just making things *more* complicated? If that's the way it seems, then it's time for some more *order*.

What Now?

First things first: "What do I do *now*?"

You can't achieve *that* goal without first reaching *this* one. Jessie probably can't get to "have more money" (goal *H*1) without first reaching "get a job" (goal *H*4). If graduating from school is a goal, then you have to go to school. If you have to go to school on a winter's morning, you first have to get dressed warmly. If you want to get dressed in an orderly fashion, you'll put your pants on before you put on your heavy boots.

"A journey of a thousand miles must begin with a single step" the Chinese philosopher Lao-Tzu pointed out 2,500 years ago. In other words, to achieve big results, you need only succeed at a series of small efforts.

With that kind of "order" in mind, Jessie can rethink her goals in terms of subgoals, or stepping-stones.

For instance, Jessie hopes to "be a better person"—which probably also means "feel better about myself." She's realized that she won't get there by wishing, dreaming, or waiting, so she's set some more concrete goals for herself, and now she's ready to think about some realistic steps toward them.

Or, to reach *her* important "Want to" goal ("look better"), Jessie's list of steps might include spending more money on clothes and taking more time getting dressed.

Steps she could take toward her "Have to" goal of "have more money" might include saving more, spending less, and getting another baby-sitting client. She could "have more time" by getting up earlier or eliminating some of her activities.

She says she "Ought to" help her mother more around the house, so she might spend more time doing chores or really making an effort to keep her room tidy.

When she plugs in her subgoals, her GO chart looks like this:

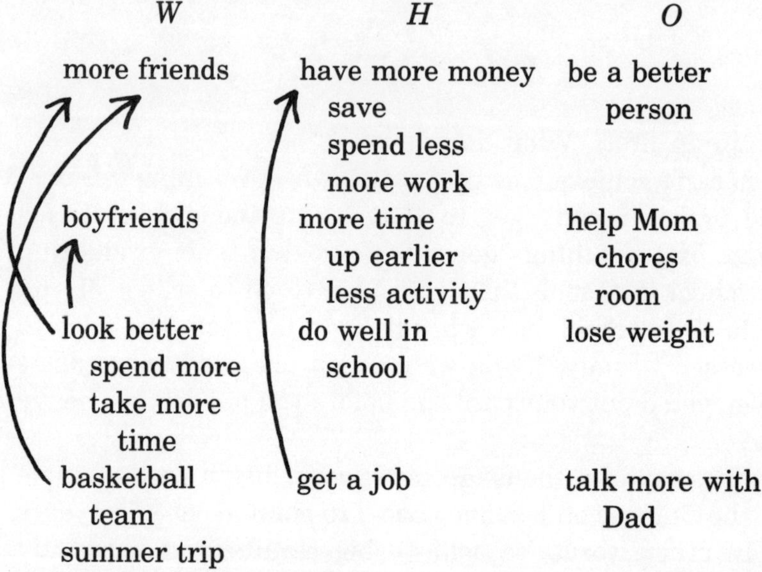

But wait a minute! Look at all those goals and subgoals that conflict with one another: spending more money on clothes but saving money; eliminating activities but adding baby-sitting and household chores.

Help! First aid: simplify.

What's the simplest way she can:

1. look better?
2. have more money and more time?
3. help her mother?

A simple solution? For one thing, Jessie can reorganize her closet! That will satisfy all three goals.

1. Her clothes will stay nicer-looking and she can see what she has so it will be easier to assemble new, snappier outfits.
2. By creating new combinations and wearing things she hasn't even been able to find in a long time, she will have a "new" wardrobe without spending any money. Plus, getting dressed each morning will take less time, leaving more time for more interesting things.
3. Her mother will be thrilled by her room.

By taking this single step, Jessie has already begun to feel better about herself . . . and all by asking, "What's the simplest solution?"

Lao-Tzu had no idea that he would set Jessie off on an important journey by helping her find the simple, single step of cleaning her closet. But he was right about a journey or goal being a step-by-step process. And this is what good organization is for: to set manageable goals that will allow you to attain grander ones, step by step.

The most important step toward any goal is the first one, and we can better decide which is first when we answer the question, When?

STRATEGY 2. COUNTDOWN

Having a clear view of your goals is important, but the trick is, of course, that whether a goal is major or minor, your efforts toward it must be made in time and in sequence.

Jake would achieve little if he applied to college right now; but if he doesn't submit his applications *in time,* he'll be out of luck, too.

Packing a suitcase just right may be a great achievement,

but not if you do it so late that you miss the train or so early that you have to unpack those items you still need on a daily basis before you leave.

If Jessie decides to rearrange all of her winter clothes just as the weather is getting hot, she's wasting a lot of time.

"Scheduling" sounds so tedious—yet we all live by schedules. Getting your homework done in time to watch your favorite TV show, putting the food in the microwave in time for it to cook so that you can eat before you go to practice, buying a birthday present before the birthday—all of these simple tasks involve scheduling.

And they all illustrate how timing can put simplicity, order, and step-by-step actions into our activities. Yet time—the ticking of that clock—still makes us tense.

Working with Time

"I've gotta get it done in time!" If that sentence alone makes you feel panicky, it's because it's the cry of someone *battling* with time, working *against* the clock. A procrastinator like Marvin eventually has to meet a deadline, so he periodically goes into a flurry of frantic activity. An overdoer like Marilyn may feel frantic all the time because she doesn't know how to pace herself.

It's easy, though, to put time on your side—and when you do, you'll find that you have a lot more of it. When you work *with* time, you can do everything *in* time.

In time means "on time"—meeting a deadline. The tidiest-looking organizational system isn't any good if it doesn't consider deadlines. Apply the *now* test: What must be done right *now?* By tonight? This week? Next year? Jessie *has to* get her paper done by Friday, so she'll need to *count down* from this deadline to pace her time properly. Jake's career dreams won't come true for years—but today he'd better study his chemistry as part of his effort toward those dreams.

In time also means "in sequence." It's easy to see that putting on hiking boots before putting on jeans goes against all the guidelines for simplicity, order, and step-by step actions. And so do these: Jessie buys new beachwear before she decides where she's going and plans to pay for travel expenses by borrowing money against her summer-job income before she gets a job.

In time can also mean "little by little." Does Jessie need to reorganize her closet in one afternoon? She can if she likes, and it makes sense if it fits with the other goals she wants to reach today or this week. But she can also do a little bit each day for a week. Marvin may discover that his life is more comfortable if he works on projects a bit at a time rather than putting it all off until the last minute.

In time can even mean "sometime" or "someday." That's the procrastinator's favorite word, but it also helps the over-doer. As soon as Marilyn hears about a project, she starts on it—so she's always overwhelmed. If Jake devotes all of his mental energy to "someday," he misses out on today.

You get the point: To achieve any goal in a simple, orderly, step-by-step way, you need to put it "in time"—into the context of time—and into a time sequence.

Timing Yourself

When must this be done? is the simple timing question.

That can mean, How much time is there? When you're starting an exam, you need to know how much time is allowed so that you can pace yourself well enough to answer all the questions.

If you have guests coming to your party at eight o'clock and it's now four o'clock, you count down and know you have four hours to get ready—or, if you've done your planning, to *finish* getting ready.

If your plane leaves at five o'clock, you can put time on your side by working backward from that deadline to schedule your pre-trip activities for the day.

That kind of time thinking works just as well with larger projects. Organizing our efforts toward any of our goals becomes much simpler when we ask, When must it be done?

Goals sort themselves into these time frames:

immediate goal—now
short-range goal—pretty soon
medium-range goal—keep it in mind
long-range goal—later
dream goal—someday

Jake's dream goals include "being happy" and "having a big career"; one long-range goal toward that end is "graduating from a good college"; for the medium-range, he can focus on "getting good grades" and "saving some money"; short-range goals include getting a job; and his immediate goal is to get a good grade on those quizzes. Jake can start a "future" shelf on his bookcase, where he keeps college catalogs, knowing that there's time to read them when he's not engaged in other necessary activities.

You can see how much simpler life becomes when goals are sorted into time frames. Timing makes it easier to get organized because you know what to do now and what to do later.

Arranging your goals into time frames helps put time on your side. It also helps you to see what sequence your efforts should take.

Do you try to meet new people before you plan a party? Or do you plan a party so that you can meet new people?

Do you save money so that you can take a trip? Or do you travel to a place where you can make money?

Does Marilyn really have to write all of her papers this

week? Maybe she does, if she knows that for three weeks next month the school fair will really take all of her time. Or does a look at her time frame show that she can write her papers one at a time over the course of the term, allowing her more time for fun in between?

Blocking out a few intensive "do-it-*now*" tasks before a big project and limiting herself to those tasks would help, as would setting deadlines for herself so that she's not working all the time.

When Jessie makes a chart according to time frames, she can see clearly what she needs to do this week. Take a look at her GO chart on page 46 and you will, too.

When you think of your own goals as a sequence of medium-range objectives that will take you step by step toward your long-range ones, GOing for what you want seems a lot more possible.

When you think of time as a matter of scheduling instead of as being a drag, it can help you work toward your goals *and* have time (and money) left over. Ready to try? Good—get set.

STRATEGY 3. TAKEOFF

Now you're getting organized!

You see *what* you want to, have to, or ought to achieve: the goals you're aiming for.

And see *when* to do it: Now? Soon? Later? Someday?

Now for the *how*.

Whether you're taking a trip, cleaning your closet, studying for exams, or campaigning for class president, you are free to choose your own *how*—your own strategy and procedure.

To reorganize a closet, some people hire experts. Jessie doesn't need that. Nor does she need to buy a closet organizer

Goal Time Frame	Want to	Have to	Ought to
Dream by: ?	be a better person ———————		
Long-range by: (date)	travel	more money	get along with family
Medium-range by: (date)	more friends boyfriends	career school success	help Mom more talk more with Dad
Short-range by: (date)	look better basketball team	job/s save $	clean room see Dad
Immediate by: Friday	practice hair call friends start diet	hustle baby-sitting study-quizes start paper	groceries Nathan call Dad

that gives equal space to dresses, skirts, and blouses. Since she doesn't have to get dressed up very often, she can put dressy clothes at the back, or up high—though someone like her mother has to keep office clothes handy. People who take pride in having closets that are color-coordinated and pretty to look at might first empty out the space, then paint it and install fancy shelf paper. Jessie doesn't care—she just wants a usable closet.

How does one get from Chicago to San Diego? Someone with a fear of flying might choose ground transportation. Others might fly, to save time; still others might choose to drive in order to see the sights.

How about you?

Set Your Course

Who you are will influence the way you go about reaching your goals in time, so think about these questions.

When you finish a project, do you:
   A. enjoy the satisfaction of finishing it?
   B. move immediately to the next project?
If you had a three-week vacation, would you:
   A. spend it at the beach?
   B. spend it traveling around the country?
Is your dream goal:
   A. concrete and specific (like "have more money")?
   B. a state of being ("be a better person")?
Do you:
   A. always have more goals than you can reach?
   B. get moving when inspiration hits?
Is it more important to you:
   A. to finish a project at any cost?
   B. to use time and patience to get it right?

If most of your answers are *A,* you are *goal-oriented*—you like getting things done.

B answers mean that you are more *process-oriented*—you enjoy the activity at least as much as the result.

When you put this information together with what you learned from the questionnaire on page 21, you have a pretty good idea of how *you* use time.

And when you combine this knowledge with the kinds of goals you set for yourself, you'll be comfortable setting workable priorities for yourself.

Goals + Time = Priorities

When you add "what to do" and "when to do it," you'll have a pretty good idea of how to go about it: Your priorities will become clear.

Some things will take priority because they are most urgent—they need to be done first or immediately. Today, Jessie's quiz is her first priority. Next week's history test is a bigger deal, but it won't be a priority.

Or something can take priority because it is most important—a "want" to be met above all others. Getting into a good college is Jake's first priority.

A priority is, most simply, something that must come prior to something else—a goal that must be met before another can be met. Having the money to pay for the ticket takes priority over a trip. Beating egg whites takes priority over making a soufflé. Saving a file takes priority over turning off the computer. Keeping your eye on the ball takes priority over hitting it.

Priorities help you take action in a simple, orderly, and step-by-step manner.

As with goals, only *you* can set your priorities. A goal-oriented person like Jake thinks in terms of getting out of high school as quickly as possible. Someone like Marvin, who enjoys hanging out and taking it easy, won't go out of his way to hurry the process of getting out of school.

And as with goals, the priorities you set depend on factors other than your own whim. There are "ought tos" and "have tos" to consider as well as "want tos," and they often take priority. Jake enjoys math; he can get lost in unraveling formulas and finding elegant solutions to complicated problems. When he's taking a math test, though, the "ought tos" and "have tos" of timing and accuracy take priority over the "want tos" of enjoying the process.

As you can imagine, when "want tos" *always* take priority over "ought tos," we don't GO very far toward our goals. So we give *first priority*—first place—to some "have tos" as a way of getting to the "want to" goals. In order to buy the things she wants to have, Jessie gives first priority to the extra hours she'll have to work.

Choosing a course to follow from among all the possibilities requires making *decisions*. "Deciding" sounds heavy: "Do I accept this college offer or that one?" So we may think that decisions are things that take a lot of effort or that should be put off indefinitely.

In fact, we make decisions almost every second. They can be as trivial as, "Do I take a bite of the meat loaf or the potatoes or both?" "Do I smile at this guy or not?" "Do I carry an umbrella or not?"

Making even the most minor decision, setting the most nearly invisible priorities, is a simple, orderly, step-by-step process involving your values, tactics, and facts.

Deciding anything big or small requires the assigning of *values* (What's important to me? Do I mind being weighed down by an umbrella? Do I mind getting wet?); a decision about *tactics* (How best can I achieve what is important to me? Should I plan to buy or borrow an umbrella if it rains?); and a gathering of *facts* (Is rain predicted for today?).

Jake wants to get decent grades because he values higher

education even more than he values being a baseball star. Using GO techniques, he gathers facts and develops tactics that will help him order his priorities to accomplish the most doable goals within his time frame.

When Jessie's goals of "look better," "have more money," and "have more time" are clear, she can see that spending more money on clothes or more time on her makeup will create conflicts. So her decisions on priorities—on goals that will lead to other goals—become much simpler, and she can arrive at the solution of reorganizing her closet.

Some priorities are imposed on us, like Jessie's quiz or her mother's expectations of her. But usually, we have to order our priorities ourselves. That means clearing away distractions that will keep us from devoting the necessary attention to a priority goal. (You may decide to clean your room when your priority should be to study for your French exam).

What if Jessie wants to diet but also wants to have lunch with her friends? Or if she wants to go to the party *and* see her dad? Then she has to do her own priority setting.

When Jessie has ordered her priorities, her GO chart will look like the one on page 51.

With this kind of clear "map" to read, Jessie is ready to GO: to make a specific plan for her day, her week, her semester.

So are you—and the next section will suggest techniques for putting these principles and strategies into use.

But before reading that, go through the next few pages to try out how far you've come already and to take some time to practice your new skills.

TRY IT!

To give you an idea of the varied ways that the S–O–S system can A–C–T, page 52 shows some examples of people GOing for very different goals.

Goal Time Frame	Want to	Have to	Ought to
Dream by: ?	be a better person ———		
Long-range by: (date)	travel	more money	get along with family
Medium-range by: (date)	more friends boyfriends	career school success	(help Mom more) talk more with Dad
Short-range by: (date)	(look better) basketball team	job/s (save $)	clean room see Dad
Immediate by: Friday	practice hair *call friends start diet	hustle baby-sitting *study-quizzes *start paper	*groceries Nathan call Dad

*Ann dreams of being a doctor—a medical missionary, help-
ing the world's peoples. Everything she does, from her schoolwork through her after-school activities, to her reading and
even TV-watching, focuses on that goal—even though she
knows that achieving it will entail a lot of hard work and
expense.*

*Mike has no such grand ideas: He just wants to get his
English paper in on time. And he has no idea of how he'll
even get to school because his car won't run.*

Kay thinks a little travel would be fun. . . .

Let's look at Kay first.

Kay's dream goal is **to travel**. To make that dream come
true, she needs to apply A–C–T: She needs to narrow her
big goal down to some manageable objectives. Writing her
goals on a GO chart will help turn her faraway dream into
next summer's reality. You can take a look at her chart on
page 53.

Aim

Kay would really like "to see the world," but she's simplified
that goal by thinking through "W–H–O says." This has helped
her decide to visit her aunt in Minnesota because she *wants
to* get away, she *has to* go somewhere cheap, and she *ought
to* visit her aunt.

So she begins to aim toward her *long-range goal* of a trip
to Minnesota.

When will she go? She "wants to" go in August because
it's hottest at home then and cooler in Minnesota—and it
will give her a vacation between her summer job and her
return to school. Besides, her aunt will be away for part of
that month, so Kay can stay at her aunt's house and use
her car for part of her vacation, and that will save money

Goal Time Frame	W	H	O
Dream by: ?	TRAVEL ————		
Long-range by: (date)	get away		visit Aunt M.
Medium-range by: (date)			
Short-range by: (date)	clothes	job	save $
*Immediate by: Friday	find travel info.	Aunt M.	exam plan

*Immediate priority list: "To dos"

write Aunt M.
reservations
job
exams, paper
shop
pack

while filling that "ought to" of seeing something of her aunt.

August is five months away, so now she has a medium-range goal to aim for: She will need X dollars for the trip—that is, if she makes her plane reservations soon to get the cheapest fare. On the other hand, once she's made her reservations, she can't change them without paying a penalty. Kay has Y dollars in her savings account that she hasn't committed to other uses, so her short-range goal becomes collecting the rest of the money. This means she needs to Aim toward a high-paying summer job.

Countdown

Now Kay begins to Count down. Will she be able to put together the remaining money in time? She has to know soon in order to take advantage of those lower fares. So she must time.

Between now and the end of school, she can work extra hours in her weekend job and make Z dollars. Will she be able to do that and avoid conflicts—that is, still have time for schoolwork and some relaxation? She can if she schedules herself carefully. And because she has only two weeks to meet the low-fare deadline, that's how long she has to line up a summer job that will pay for the trip.

Once that's done, she can make her reservations and put the countdown on hold for a while. She knows she has some subgoals to aim for: putting together a travel wardrobe, for instance, and reading up on the special sights and events in her aunt's part of Minnesota.

She'll have plenty of time to do that during the next few months, but . . .

Takeoff

. . . if Kay wants a successful Takeoff, she'll need to set some priorities. Setting priorities means balancing goals with time. That wardrobe, for instance: She wants a nice one, but she also wants a good chunk of travel money. So, rather than buying a new bathing suit now, she decides to wait for the sales later in the summer.

Step by step, in simple, orderly fashion, she's moving toward her goal. As her departure date nears, the countdown picks up speed, and her priorities become getting her stuff together and figuring out how to get to the airport in time for the actual takeoff.

By aiming, counting down, and setting priorities for her takeoff, Kay will achieve her current goal of getting to Minnesota—and she'll also have practiced some important techniques for reaching her dream goal "to see the world." In fact, she's probably learned that the A–C–T strategies work for achieving *any* goal.

They work for Ann, the future missionary, too, by helping her **plan her future**. Watch!

Aim

On her GO chart, Ann has written her dream goal, and she has also noted her:

- long-range goals of medical and divinity school.
- medium-range goal of a good premed religious college.
- short-range goals of good grades and relevant volunteer work.
- immediate goals of acing the exam and finding three hours on Saturday to spend at the hospital.

Countdown

Now it will be easy to set the clock toward her goal. She'll find out when she starts high school what courses she needs to take if she wants to be accepted as a premed. She'll start to find out about and visit colleges by about her junior year.

And she'll give herself plenty of time to fill out those college applications at the beginning of her senior year.

Takeoff

Now Ann needs to decide *how* to set her course. Her goals-plus-time priorities make it simple. With her GO chart on her wall, she can see the direct connection between studying for chemistry this week and becoming a medical missionary someday.

A–C–T simplifies Mike's dilemma, too, and helps put things into step-by-step order. His aim is to get **a school paper done on time,** so he'll count down for takeoff from that due date. Since he can always hitch a ride to school, getting his car fixed has a much lower priority.

You, too, can use the A–C–T strategies on *any* project you "want to" or "have to" do. Just remember: To Get Set, you must take Simple, Orderly Steps to Aim for your goals (decide *what* to do), Count down from a deadline (decide *when* to do it), and Take off toward your priorities (figure out *how* to go about it). *What* plus *when* equals *how*—it's that simple.

But what *are* you aiming for?

Why not make your own GO chart and take a look. It's easy. Take the list of goals you jotted down at the beginning of this chapter and read them over again. Do they still look right? Are there some goals you might add or take away?

Now pick up your pad and pencil and make a GO chart like the one Jessie drew on page 46. Insert the goals you listed.

Once you've laid them out so that you can see them clearly, are there any you want to add to or take away from your list?

What subgoals lead to other goals? Draw arrows between those.

What will you GO for first? What are your priorities? Circle them.

Now you can see what *you* are Going for. Interesting, isn't it? At the beginning of this chapter, you may not have even known you had any goals—or you thought you had so many that you'd never be able to reach them. Now you have a clearer picture of what you "want to," "have to," and "ought to" do— and *when* to do it.

The next chapter will give you techniques on *how* to go about doing it.

THREE

ACTION!

The Three Techniques to GO for It:

Write-up—Backup—Letup

So far, getting organized hasn't been so tough, has it? All you need are the GO principles (Simplicity, Order, Steps) and the strategies to put them to use (set the goals to Aim for, set the clock to Countdown, and set a course for Takeoff).

You've put together a GO chart that maps your goals and the general route to follow toward them.

Now for the *techniques* to convert your goals into an action plan, a plan that works for *you* and that will help you work toward your goals. Take your GO chart and pin it to your bulletin board, tape it to your wall or mirror, or clip it in the back of your notebook. That way, you'll have a handy reminder of what *you* want to GO for.

The planning techniques you'll find in this chapter aren't just master plans for major life issues. Planning is simply thinking ahead. It works just as well for getting through a busy day, organizing a party, or mapping out a trip. It works for anything you "want to," "have to," or "ought to" GO for today, this week, this month, or this year.

These tips work because you will be picking the tips that work for *you*. Just as your goals, your timetable, and your priorities are your own, so is your planning system. A plan is no good unless you are comfortable enough with it to use it automatically. Otherwise, it just gets in your way.

For instance, Jessie's friend Sue is planning a trip, too. She got a file folder with lots of pockets, labeled each pocket with one stop on her planned tour, and put guidebooks and other information about that spot into each of its pockets. She will take the folder with her. As she travels, her references will be handy, and before she leaves each site, she will replace the guides in the folder with souvenirs. To some people, that system may seem brilliant, but to Jessie, it makes travel seem as exciting as sorting socks.

Or there's Jake's friend Sam, who never takes notes in class and rarely writes his assignments down. Somehow, he must keep all his learning and his "to dos" in his head because he's done all right in school. But this technique appeals to Jake about as much as walking a tightrope over a pit of poisonous snakes.

Sue's system works for her, and Sam's system works for him.

Whatever *your* style, you'll find here some simple, orderly, step-by-step techniques for planning action. They help you make an action plan because change and flexibility are built into them.

TECHNIQUE 1. WRITE-UP

Here are some simple-sounding ways to remember a bunch of things:

- Count off all the "to dos" on your fingers. If you know you have, say, five things to remember, you'll have an easy time working through all of them.
- Group all your "to dos" by category ("homework," "chores," "phone calls," and so on). When you remember the category, the details will come to you.
- Use gimmicks like abbreviations and code words (S–O–S, A–C–T, and "W–H–O says" are ones that should sound familiar by now), or rhymes, rhythms, or melodies. Put the day's responsibilities into a poem or a song, and you can hum your way straight through.

In addition to these suggestions, there's one really simple way to remember most of your activities: Write them down!

Write-Ups: the S–O–S Way to A–C–T

Putting down your plans and schedules in writing is a lot simpler than carrying around everything in your head. We all have more than one goal to GO for, more than one activity going on at a time, and our involvement in them is enough to think about without also having to remember when to pick up the laundry or what day to register for gym class.

When you're baking a cake, writing a paper, or building or repairing anything, you know the project becomes much simpler when you set the ingredients, notes, parts, and instructions out within easy sight and reach. Writing down your activities and assignments serves the same purpose: It simplifies your time by "laying it out"—on paper—within easy sight and reach.

Using a calendar or date book to order your activities helps you not only to schedule your time but to find more of it. Even if you're not the "schedule" type, try keeping a time record for a week or two: Note on a pocket calendar or pad how much time and which hours you spend on each activity—homework, dressing, eating, hanging out—each day. Then look at it carefully. No matter how busy and pressured and overwhelmed you think you are, you'll probably find that there are pieces of time you could use better. Doing some homework on the bus home or reviewing class notes while you're eating breakfast, for instance, can actually improve your efficiency—and give you more time for the things you really want to do.

You'll also be able to pinpoint areas where you spend too much time unnecessarily. That way you'll know that when you need to find some extra time fast, you can "find" it in the hours you spend on the phone or in the minutes you spend ironing a shirt that wouldn't have been wrinkled if it had been hung up.

A Write-up that's right for you will help bring order to your life by showing:

> how much time there is.
> how much time each activity takes.
> when each must be finished.

It will also give you a way to hang on to your time because it becomes a diary or memory book of how you've spent your recent months and years.

Writing up your activities also helps you go through them step by step: An annual calendar reminds you to plan ahead for big events; a schedule for your week helps you set your priorities day by day; party-planning or suitcase-packing lists make sure you don't forget the ice or the underwear.

Simple Tools

Your Write-ups can take any form you like so long as they're simple for *you* to use.

You can spend a lot of money on a beautiful leather-bound

diary, just make a list each week on a piece of scrap paper, or pick any kind of notebook in between. You can find software for your computer that will schedule your life or buy an electronic pocket calendar/notebook that enables you to punch in everything you need to do or to know wherever you are.

Just look for a format that enables you to lay out the day, the week, the month, and the year ahead in a way that will make it comfortable for you to think ahead and remember; to simplify your activities and eliminate the unnecessary; and to find time, make time, and use time to your best advantage.

Go to a stationery store and browse through all the possibilities until you find a calendar, date book, or notebook that seems to fit your needs. Don't spend a lot at first because you may decide you need something different. Some calendars begin the year with January while some academic-year calendars start with September and run through the school year plus the summer; some show a month per page, some a week, some a day; and calendars come in all shapes, sizes, and prices. You can also simply get a pocket memo pad and use it to jot down your activities—a day, a week, or an event per page. Small "stick-on" pads are useful, too; use them to insert a list of "to dos" in your notebook or on your calendar, and toss the list when you're done.

Whatever style you pick, get two planners (but no more than two): one that is small and lightweight enough to carry with you in your pocket, purse, backpack, or notebook; and one for your wall or desk that shows a whole month or year at a time and is big enough for you to write on. If you have one at home and one that's portable—and you keep both up-to-date—you won't "lose your life" if you lose your pocket planner.

Why no more than two? Because, while having your list with you is convenient and having it spread out in your room gives you the big picture, having to make notes on more than two complicates, rather than simplifies, your life. Some people might want a separate assignment book for classes, but making space for these notations and jotting down miscellaneous memos and ideas in your pocket calendar works just as well and lessens your load.

Ordering Your Time

And now, to *use* these tools. Each of us has a different style. Some prize neatness over speed and write careful, detailed memoranda, even using different-colored inks for different categories. Others jot down hasty notes in a code that only they can understand, using hasty circles, lines, arrows, and exclamation points for messy emphasis.

Use whatever style works for you, and it *will* work if you remember S–O–S and think of your activities in the context of their time frames: dream goals, long-range goals, medium-range goals, short-range goals, and immediate goals.

Dream goals belong in a special place: on your wall, on your mirror, on a bulletin board next to your GO chart, or, perhaps, in a separate notebook or folder on a shelf. They will stay there—and in the back of your mind—as you focus on your day-to-day activities. When you get an idea, or read something that relates to your dream goals, put it with your "dreams." That keeps it fresh. Jake has a shelf in his room where he keeps college catalogs and car magazines. Marilyn keeps a "to do" looseleaf notebook, divided into sections, so she won't have to be *thinking* constantly about all she has to do.

Every now and then, you'll want to think about your dream goals. You'll want to alter them, perhaps—or take notes of where you are in relation to them—and rearrange your GO chart somewhat as a result. Pencil in a date next to these dreams and their alterations. As time goes by, you may be surprised at how solid—or changeable—those dreams are.

Long-range goals need attention well in advance. At the

beginning of each year or school year, go through the whole calendar or date book and mark important, fixed dates like birthdays and school breaks. It's a good idea to use pencil for all but the absolute certainties—like fixed holidays, birthdays, or term beginnings and endings. Erasing changes as you move objectives from place to place throughout the year makes for less confusion.

Put in advance reminders, too: A month or so before a special birthday, for instance, note, "Plan party"; a couple of months before summer vacation, write, "Find summer job." This technique helps someone like Marilyn to remember that she doesn't have to do everything at once—and it reminds Marvin to take a few small steps ahead of deadline times.

In your first classes of the semester, note the dates for final exams and term papers due, and jot down advance reminders for those, too. As you hear about parties, club meetings, dances, games, team tryouts, doctor appointments, or other special events, note them on the appropriate page—and be sure to mark them on your at-home calendar, too.

Your medium-range goals fit in to the long-range ones. When a month is nearing its end, flip to the next one. Check what's coming up, cross off or erase cancellations and changes, and make additions. Especially note such high-priority items as application deadlines or interview dates.

Block out do-it-*now* times when you'll really focus all your energy on one project. This is particularly important for someone who has more than three things going on at once (and who doesn't?). When you have three papers due in the same week, for instance, you'll need to set your *own* deadlines: Schedule yourself to finish them at different times, no matter when you have to turn them in.

Short-range planning brings your focus to the *now*—but it's more effective if that *now* is a week or a day at a time instead of moment to moment. Before each week begins, plan your play, work, and study time by marking it off on your calendar or listing it in your notebook. Each evening, you may want to make a list of the next day's activities so that you'll be free to go through them without spending time thinking about them.

Jessie's day and week got a lot simpler to manage when she got in the habit of spending a few minutes on Sunday thinking ahead to the week and jotting down "to do" notes for the week of things to do each day. And by preparing on Monday night for the events of Tuesday, she avoided a lot of hassle.

Another way to get organized for the short term, whether it's a day or an individual project, is to literally lay out what you'll need. Just as Jessie can hang tomorrow's clothes in an easy-to-see spot, you can make a separate space for stacking or arranging the *stuff* that goes into a term paper, a hobby activity, or the like. That way, it's always handy when you need it and in view as a reminder.

Listing the Steps

Whether it's sewing, building, learning a new computer program, or cooking, most activities come with step-by-step instructions. In the same way, you provide "instructions" for yourself when you make a list.

Once you've gotten to the *now* of your plans, you need to pay close attention to all the things you have to do today or for a specific project like planning a party or writing a paper.

When you make a list, brainstorm: Write down everything that comes to mind on the topic. Then you can organize it by grouping similar items together or arranging it in order of sequence or time frames.

Does all of this Write-up effort sound like a lot more planning than you have time for? Once you try it, you'll find that it *makes* more time and actually gives you more freedom. Writing up not only organizes your activities so that you needn't always be thinking about what must be done but also warns you when you have too much on the agenda— *before* you get deep into the overwhelmed state that exhausts the overdoer and paralyzes the procrastinator.

TECHNIQUE 2. BACKUP

All these GO techniques should make life tidy, right? Everything is laid out according to simple, orderly steps. The goals are there, and the timing, so you go ahead and act . . . and then what? Does even perfect planning guarantee success? No. The trouble is, life doesn't always happen according to plan or schedule. That's why every plan needs a Backup.

With a Backup, you are *guaranteed* success, because not only will you have a Plan *B* to fall back on, but you'll also see how a flexible approach can help you to succeed even when you don't reach every goal you GO for perfectly.

Relist

You'll see that some Backup is built right in to the plans you've already made if you just back up and take a look.

What happens if you look at your list, your calendar, or your date book and realize that there's just too much on it? A Tuesday that lists six hours of study simply won't fit into a day that includes seven hours of school, three hours of work, two hours of travel time, and about three hours for telephoning, eating, dressing, and the like. The three hours that would be left over for sleep are simply not enough for that kind of day!

What if you see that you have three exams this week, you're on the decoration committee for Friday's dance, you've promised to see your little sister's school play, and you're about to take a baby-sitting job? Burnout!

What if your "big goals" for the year are to make the varsity, run for class president, get all *A*s, and earn enough money to buy a car? Pretty high expectations!

So what do you do in situations like these? *Simplify!*

Take a step back. Take another look at your list or calendar, and take it apart. Give each item the "W–H–O says" test: Is this a "want to," a "have to," or an "ought to"? How important is it? "W–H–O says?" And for each item, ask:

> *Must* it be done?
> Must it be done *now*?
> Must it be done now *by me*?

Then take away each item that deserves an *honest* "No" to these questions.

Taking it step by step, relist. Reorganize your list by putting some of it off until Wednesday and skipping the lowest-priority items; e.g., cut down on phoning or skip baby-sitting this week. Focus on the high-priority items—like short-range school assignments. All those big goals won't disappear, but pick only two to really work at.

List leftovers—buying dance decorations or outlining your term paper, for instance—make excellent "instant backups." What's left over after you've managed the top-priority items from Plan *A* become Plan *B* and turn into the priority items on the next Plan *A*.

Crossing items off in advance is like preventive medicine. When the best-laid plans *don't* work out, you'll continue to have success if you think "backup" as first aid for this "disaster."

And don't forget to congratulate yourself for what you *have* accomplished.

Sometimes when we can't do everything, we feel as though we've done nothing. But it's only natural that we can't always meet all of our goals—so . . .

Replan

What if you get sick two days before your big party? What if Jake doesn't get into the college of his choice—or if he does and finds out he hates it? What if Jessie doesn't make enough money in time for her trip?

When plans don't work out, is it a disaster? Have you failed? What do you do?

Well, you can try to alter reality so you can continue with your original plans—that's a sure recipe for panic and paralysis.

Or you can replan, and alter your plans to fit reality: Postpone the party until you're well; find another college; or take daytrips to the beach and save the extra money.

It's easy to know how to change plans or directions when you have your goals clearly in mind—or on paper. Is it more important to have the party now or to have the party when you can enjoy it? To have a satisfying life or to stick rigidly to a plan you no longer want? Replanning requires as much personal decision making as does planning.

Rethink and Relax

Sometimes we bend over backward so far to stick to our plans that we defeat the whole purpose. If Kay is determined to take exactly the trip she's planned, she may end up not going anywhere.

Instead of bending over backward so far that you fall, back up your plans with flexibility. Though you don't want to clutter up your mind—or your lists—with every possible "what if," it's good to keep in mind that if one plan doesn't work out, another will. When you're feeling under pressure from your "to dos," ask yourself, "What's the worst that can happen if I don't achieve this?" It's a good way to keep your priorities in order, and it can be relaxing to realize that life will go on and new plans will come up.

If something on Tuesday's list doesn't get done, do you stay up late to do it just because you've put it on the list? Of course not.

Just because you "want to" or "ought to" do something, do you "have to" do it? *Now?*

Just because you don't accomplish something *now,* does it mean you never will?

No. Flexibility is an excellent backup: If you stay loose physically you're less likely to get hurt in a fall. In the same way, if you're flexible in your planning, you will always have a safe fallback because a fallback from Plan *A* to Plan *B* isn't failure, but a different kind of success.

TECHNIQUE 3. LETUP

Sometimes, the best Backup technique is knowing when to Let up on a project or on yourself. What if, no matter how hard you try, no matter what you do, you can't get to your goal? Even if that goal is as simple as getting through all the items on your list for the day, not reaching it can be frustrating.

When faced with frustration, whether major or minor, remember what you learned back at the beginning of the book, "If it's not simple, something's wrong."

Simplify by taking a look to see what is wrong: Are there too many things on your list? Are your goals in conflict? Is it just that you don't have enough information or other (more personal) resources to do what needs to be done?

If an army battalion is engaged in an assault that was carefully planned but is not getting near its objective and is taking a lot of casualties, does it keep at it until every soldier is dead? No—it retreats and regroups for a different kind of assault.

Overdoers will keep at a set of projects until they literally drop and can't go for anything more. Fiercely goal-oriented types will go for one goal so hard they can't change direction and go for anything else. If you are like either of these types, or if you just have too much to do, simplify by doing just *one* task today. Tomorrow will be easier.

When you run up against a brick wall in your plans, do you keep beating your head against it—or do you stop?

Fed Up?

In GOing for anything, it's important to know when and how to STOP—to know when you've had enough.

The following are some indications that you've had enough, temporarily or permanently, in work on a single project or a major goal:

- *The losing-it stage.* You're sewing a shirt or building a loft bed and you keep losing the scissors or the hammer or making other mistakes. . . . You're writing a paper and you keep losing your notes or your train of thought. . . . You're creating a program and almost hit the key that will lose the whole thing forever. . . . You've lost sight of why you're doing all this work in the first place. . . . You're emotionally "losing it" and snapping at friends and family.

When you reach this stage on a big or a little project, STOP. You won't go anywhere but backward. At best, you'll foul up the project at hand.

- *The "I'm-bored" stage.* All of a sudden, everything you're doing, today or this year, seems like a total drag. Maybe you're just tired or overwhelmed—or maybe the goal you're working toward has lost its appeal. STOP. Step back and rethink. Maybe you should change your goal or your planning toward it. Some goals—like writing the paper or keeping at the job you're getting paid for—you can't abandon no matter how boring they seem. But boredom is a signal to stop at least for a little while, because if you're working at something that really bores you, it won't turn out well.

- *The "I-can't-do-anything!" stage.* What this really means is that you can't do *every*thing! Procrastinators and overdoers alike sometimes feel so overwhelmed by everything they have to do (no matter how well it's organized) that they're in danger of total collapse. This is the time to STOP doing "everything" and focus on getting *one* thing done *now*. Or make up your mind that if you achieve one objective today, you have succeeded.

- *The "I'm-just-too-tired" stage.* This can be another way of saying, "I'm overwhelmed" or "I'm bored." But maybe you really *are* tired. Managing all you have to manage can be tiring and stressful. If you're tired all the time, if you can't sleep or if you want to sleep all the time, if you're eating oddly to "get energy," or if you're using caffeine or other drugs to keep going—STOP. These are signs of heavy stress; not only do we function poorly under stress, but, more important, *no* goal is worth getting totally stressed-out for.

When you're feeling fed up with anything, you have a much greater chance of success if, instead of going at it, you stop— at least for a while. When you've taken a long-enough and far-enough step back to see what's happening, you may pick up the project again—or you may decide to give up.

Let Go

If Jessie can't seem to lose any more weight, no matter how committed she is to her diet, does it make sense for her to make herself feel like such a failure that she binges all her weight back on? When Jake can't make the baseball team, does he feel such shame at this failure that he quits school? Giving up on a project doesn't mean failure.

If things don't seem to be going right, take it as a hint that something may be wrong

- with your plan, so take another look. (If Jessie made some extra time for herself, she could walk to school and lose weight without eating less.)
- with your goal, so take another look. ("W–H–O says" that Jake has to make the baseball team?)

Or it may simply be something intangible that says, "It wasn't meant to be."

The harder you push in a situation like this, the less likely you are to succeed. How many times have you looked for something frantically—to the point where you said, "I give up"—and then suddenly remembered where you put it?

The harder you focus on one objective, the more tightly you close your mind to other possibilities and the harder it is to achieve *any* kind of success.

In an exam, you're advised to skip over problems you just can't figure out rather than waste too much time on them.

But even though you let go of the mental struggle and move on to something else, your mind keeps playing with that insoluble problem, and you often find that if you go back to it, the answer will come to you all of a sudden.

One reason for starting papers early is that you can write a draft and put it away for a bit. If you come back to it later, you will see where you need to rewrite much more clearly than you would if you just stuck to your keyboard and kept agonizing over the draft.

So instead of hammering your head harder against whatever brick wall you find in your way, remember to take it easy—and just "give up."

"Giving up" isn't failing. It's letting go of something so that you can step back and get a new perspective on it. This may help you see a whole new line of action you'd never even thought of—a different approach or a different goal.

Think about the project and count S–O–S on your fingers. Have you made this as simple, orderly, and step-by-step as possible? Count off A–C–T. Is this a goal that makes sense? Are there others that are more important right now? Have you set a reasonable time frame and really devoted some concentrated time to it? Have you done everything you can to reach this goal?

If the answer is "yes," then you know you're better off stopping.

Don't even *call* it "giving up" or "failing." Call it what it really is: letting go.

You can completely give up on a project or you can just store it literally in the back of your mind—in one far corner of your consciousness—and go about your business. Then see if you don't get an idea about how to handle it. Who knows why this works, but it does, and it gives you reason not to be so tightly bound to your ideas and schedules.

So, if something you try is just too hard or isn't working out, STOP. Let up and let go—and you'll find that you've made room for other ideas.

Get Up and GO

Sometimes, of course, we can't get around the fact or the feeling that we have, indeed, failed in our efforts.

You want to be an actor, and you've pinned all your long-range hopes and short-range plans on getting the lead in the class play—but you don't even get past the tryouts. Jessie sleeps through her history exam. Marilyn finds she's promised to be three places at once.

Oof! These are not successful experiences. But they can help you to succeed another time if you turn them into learning experiences.

Find out where you went wrong: In the area of Simplicity, Order, Steps? In the goal you aimed for? The time you planned for it? The actions you took?

If you take a good look at where you went wrong, you'll have a better chance of going right the next time.

So take a deep breath, get up, and get going!

How?

Get out your plans and your lists, pick up a pencil with a fresh eraser, and . . .

Remember S–O–S and A–C–T: Set new goals, a new schedule, and a new action plan that will take you to success with simple, orderly steps.

Try some of the tools that are designed to give you freedom and success. Really practice the write-up–backup–letup techniques described here until you find a comfortable way to make action planning a habit.

For a start at trying it, read on.

TRY IT!

You have many tools available to help you get organized, but the cheapest, easiest, and most basic is a *list*. Lists are the Simple, Orderly, Step-by-Step way to organize anything and everything you want, from dreams of "How to Live Happily Ever After" to every color sock you want to buy. Lists work especially well for managing the matters at hand.

For example, if Margie is planning a party, watch how making a list in the right way can help her get organized by allowing her to Aim toward her goal, Count down toward the party-time deadline, and Take off for A–C–Tion. It will also show her where she really has to focus her attention and where she can Back up and Let up so that the party will be as much fun for her as for her guests.

The right way **to plan a party** is—you guessed it—the S–O–S way, so . . .

Write-up
First, *take a look:* Margie jots down (in pencil) *everything* that must be done for her party.

> invite J, K, WM, Pete, A, NP, NR, GG, plus? (25?)
> lots soda
> here? where?
> May 5? 12?
> balloons?
> inv's—surprise!
> cake?
> wear blue dress?
> music from Joey
> clean
> snax? or meal?
> get help (ask MJ)
> cost!

Second, *take apart:* She groups the items on her list by time frame or by other connections.

Do food plan invite J, K, WM, Pete, A, NP, NR, GG, plus? (25?)
lots soda
here? where?
May 5? 12?
balloons?
inv's—surprise!
food plan cake?
wear blue dress?
music from Joey
Do food plan clean
snax? or meal?
get help (ask MJ)
cost!

Third, *take away:* Margie eliminates the unnecessary items and *prioritizes* the rest according to time or importance. She may rewrite her list in priority order or just mark the various priorities with letters or numbers.

1 invite J, K, WM, Pete, A, NP, NR, GG, plus? (25?)
3 lots soda
1 here? where?
1 balloons?
1 inv's—surprise!
3 cake?
4 wear blue dress?
3 music from Joey
4 clean
3 snax? or meal?
2 get help (ask MJ)
2 cost

Backup

When Margie takes another look at her list, she finds ways to Back up (and Let up). She rethinks every item with a question mark. Which will be simpler—to have the party at her house or somewhere else? With snacks or with more elaborate food? Does she really want twenty-five people? Etc.

She'll leave some questioned items as "leftovers": Maybe she'll have time and money for balloons—maybe not; maybe she'll want to wear her blue dress—maybe not.

Letup

One item, "Get help," gives Margie the perfect way to let up on herself. After all, *she* wants to have fun, too.

Now make a list for yourself. Anything will do: a grocery list, a list of all your homework assignments for the week, a list of clothes or music you'd like to buy. Write it on your pad of paper and follow the S–O–S steps to make it as useful as possible.

If you get into the habit of carrying around a list-making kit (pencil and small paper) and of making a list of "to dos" before the week or day begins, you'll be going a long way toward getting organized.

Diaries, date books, or any kind of notebooks that are arranged by date and give you enough space for writing can be valuable tools for, in effect, juggling and combining many different lists. Margie, for example, is not only planning a party but looking for a job; preparing for finals and papers; and going through her usual round of music lessons, household chores, baby-sitting, and the like.

So for a typical week, here's how she would **use her diary.**

Write-up

As you can see from her diary on page 79, she stars or highlights the most important events and enters reminders day by day as she goes through her week step by step.

MONDAY

Mom away this week - sit Tommy.

8
9
10 (math quiz)
11
1
2
3 SC mt'g
4
5
EVE Call - party inv's ? - $?
      Aunt L. dinner

TUESDAY

8
9
10
11
   order cake ($$?)
1
2
3
4 lib. paper - meet Sam
5
EVE sit Johnsons 7:30 (study French)

WEDNESDAY

8
9
10
11 (*French test)
1
2
3
4 Game ? Lib.! gov't paper!
5
EVE do paper!

THURSDAY

8
9
10
11
         deli - job?
1
2 (gov't paper due)
3   piano lesson
4
5 pick up Mom - airport
EVE call - help Sat. & Sun.?

FRIDAY

8 → dentist!
9
10
11 gym - note ?
1
2
3 remind K - get J here late
4 grocery store...
5 dress from cleaner
EVE bake cake ? Joey - CDplayer
      clean

SATURDAY/SUNDAY

8
9
10
11 decorate (A & NP)
      clean up (MJ)
1
2 ice & soda   study Math
3 vacuum   Mon.!
4 Shower
5 hair
EVE (Party) 8PM

Backup
Look at Margie's diary on page 81, and note what has been moved around on this week's plan.

Letup
Now let's see what's been eliminated from Margie's busy week on page 82.

Planning calendars—whether they are the kind that hang on a wall or that you carry with you—fit all these activities into a larger context. They help you Write up your activities in a way that not only reminds you of things that have to be done but also gives you an overview of everything that's going on so that you know when you can—or should—Back up and Let up. Look at the one on page 83.

In short, a calendar can simplify your complicated life while, at the same time, helping you to keep in view all the goals you're GOing for.

Other tools that help you keep those goals in order are (1) notebooks, divided according to all your separate medium- and long-range goals and (2) files, boxes, or big envelopes labeled to collect your big ideas. This is where you should keep your dreams for all the ideas and plans you hope will work out someday. By organizing them, and sorting through them periodically, you can start GOing for them *now*.

What are *you* GOing for? What are some of your big dreams? They should be right there on your GO chart. Even if it's not time to take action toward them right now, start stashing them in those files for later.

What do you need to plan for today, this week, this month? Get a diary and a calendar and then make a *list* of what needs planning.

MONDAY

Mom away this week - sit Tommy.

8
9
10 (math quiz)
11

1
2
3 SC mt'g
4
5
EVE Call - party inv's ? - $?
     Aunt L. dinner

TUESDAY

8
9
10
11
    order cake ($$?)
1
2
3   Lib.
4   lib. paper - meet Sam
5
EVE sit Johnsons 7:30 (study French)
     HOME - Tommy   French - study

WEDNESDAY

8
9
10
11 (*French test)

1
2
3
4   Game ? Lib.! gov't paper!
5
EVE do paper!
     (home - Tommy)

THURSDAY

8
9
10
11
                    deli - job?
1
2 (gov't paper due)
3   piano lesson
4
5   pick up Mom - airport
EVE call - help Sat. & Sun.? sit Johnsons 7:30

FRIDAY

8 → dentist!
9
10
11 gym - note ?

1
2
3   remind K - get J here late
4   grocery store... mJ!!
5   dress from cleaner   buy cake
EVE bake cake ? Joey - CD player
     clean

SATURDAY/SUNDAY

8
9
10
11   decorate (A & NP)

         clean up (mJ)
1
2   ice & soda   study Math
3   vacuum   Mon.!
4   Shower
5   hair
EVE (Party) 8PM

MONDAY

(DO)   Mom away this week - sit Tommy. (NOTE)

8
9
(10) math quiz
11   prep gov't paper

1   party - calls
2   . B, M, & T - food, etc.
(3) SC mt'g   Joe - CD player
4   Sam?   A & N - decorate
5        $. K - J here late
(EVE) Call - party inv's ? - ?   MJ clean
Aunt L. dinner

TUESDAY — Tommy school

8
9
10
11
order cake (ff ?)
1   outline gov't paper
2
3   Lib.
(4) lib. paper - meet Sam
5
EVE sit Johnsons 7:30 (study French)
Home - Tommy   French - study

WEDNESDAY - Tommy school

8
9
10
(11) *French test
1
2
3
4   Game ? Lib.! gov't paper!
5
(EVE)   do paper!
(home - Tommy) ↓

THURSDAY - Tommy school

8   (DO)   (NOTE)
9
10
11
        deli - job?
1
(2) gov't paper due
3   piano lesson
4
5   pick up Mom - airport
EVE   call   help Sat. & Sun.? sit Johnsons 7:30

FRIDAY

8 → dentist!
9
10
11   gym - note?

1
2
3   remind K - get J here late
4   grocery store...   MJ ll
5   dress from cleaner   (buy cake)
EVE   bake cake? Joey   CD player
clean

SATURDAY/SUNDAY

8
9   decorate
10   vacuum, etc.
11   decorate (A & N)
L ice & soda   clean up (MJ)
1
2   ice & soda shower   study Math
3   vacuum hair   Mon.!
4   shower food ready
5   hair
EVE (Party) 8pm

MAY

SUN.	MON.	TUES.	WED.	THURS.	FRI.	SAT.
		1 (Mom away) home (T)	2 Tommy school French test game home (T)	3 Tommy school gov't paper	4 dentist-8 Prep party	5 PARTY
6	7 math quiz (SC)	8 sit- J's	9 game -a	10 call deli - interview?	11 Ann's birthday	12 interview - deli job
13 picnic? beach?	14 math quiz (SC)	15 sit?	16 French test game -h	17 shop with Mom	18 D A D	19
20	21 math quiz (SC)	22 sit?	23	24 French paper	25 DANCE	26 [history]
27 history review with J]	28 (SC)	29	30 hist. final	31 PREP FINALS!		

Adapt the techniques to fit your own needs and style—and remember that your goal is to keep your life as simple as possible as you Write up, Back up, and, especially, Let up. One of the most important tools you have is your*self* and your sense of what you need and can do.

You can do a lot—as you'll see for yourself in the next chapter.

FOUR

GO TO IT

Congratulations! Now you're ready . . . to take your life in your hands, to get yourself in hand, to hold any goal you want in the palm of your hand.

So count off the simple, orderly steps on the fingers of one hand.

Simplicity
Order
Steps

Use three fingers of your other hand to get set for action.

Aim
Countdown
Takeoff

That's all you need to get organized and GO for it!
So give yourself a hand, because here's what you've learned:

I. TAKE IT EASY
   The Three Principles of Good Organization
   When the going gets rough—when you can't
   seem to get where you want to GO—take the
   easy way out. On even the most frantic day,
   use this simple, three-step S–O–S system to get
   organized:

   1. Simplicity
      The hardest task, the most complicated life,
      is manageable if you keep it simple. In fact,
      "If it's not simple, something's wrong." So:
         Take a Look
         Take Apart
         Take Away
         Take Another Look
   2. Order
      The simple way to GO is:
         First Things First
   3. Steps
      The simple, orderly route to success goes
      one step at a time
         Now or Later
         Day by Day

II. GET SET
   The Three Strategies of Good Organization
   To get anywhere, you need to know where you're
   going, when you have to get there, and the short-
   est route to take. So before you GO for it, get
   set. To use the Simple, Orderly, Step-by-Step
   (S–O–S) system to A–C–T:

   1. Aim

Take aim at what you "want to," "have to," and "ought to" do, and do it.

   2. Countdown

Count down to *when* you must do it and when you *can* do it, and apply S–O–S to deadlines and schedules.

   3. Takeoff

To take off, put things in order and GO, step by step.

III. ACTION!

The Three Techniques to GO for It

Before you can GO, you've got to have a plan. But if a plan is boring, it's no good. So simplify, order, and succeed step by step with this action plan:

   1. Write-up

Make lists and plans that *you* will use for orderly, step-by-step success.

   2. Backup

Relist, replan, rethink . . . and relax.

   3. Letup

Take it easy! There's no such thing as failure, especially when you know how to use "give up" and "let up" systems to GO for it again.

Here's proof that you *can* GO for it and take it easy, too. You'll find some examples and exercises to play with, think about, and do to gain hands-on GO experience that you can apply to your own life.

It's simple—even fun. Just remember S–O–S (Simplicity–Order–Steps) and A–C–T (Aim–Countdown–Takeoff) to GO (Get Organized).

PUTTING IT ALL TOGETHER

Here's how you can **take an exam** using the GO system:

Simplicity
First, *take a look:* Read over the whole test before answering any questions. Then, *take apart:* Which sections require short answers? Essays? Which are for extra credit? Next, *take away:* If it says, "Answer two out of five" or the like, lightly (or mentally) cross out the ones you won't answer. Finally, *take another look:* Read those instructions again, quickly. And check to see that you've put your name on the test as directed.

Order
First, answer the questions you *know* you know. Focus most of your time and attention on the most important questions—usually, the ones that carry the most points. And put everything else out of your mind, including the things you studied that aren't asked for on this test.

Steps
Though the back of your mind may be chewing on the other questions you've scanned, concentrate on answering one question at a time.

Aim
Your goal is to get the best possible grade on this test. If you count on perfection or expect to fail, rethink your aim: the best *possible* grade.

Countdown

Figure how long you have for the whole test and for each section. Pay attention to the clock so you won't spend too much time on one area.

Takeoff

Give the most possible correct answers, the fullest essay, in the time allowed.

Write-up

Mark or write your answers clearly: If they can't be read, they won't be counted. Include any figuring that's asked for. If you run out of time for an essay, write an outline or a few key words.

Backup

Go back over the test, checking your answers. Rethink any you weren't sure of, and take a stab at them. Did you follow instructions? And don't forget to check your name!

Letup

When you've finished the exam, let it go. Plan to use any wrong answers as a way to help you study better for the next test. If you do get a bad grade, you can ask to make it up. If you don't understand the grade, ask about it; using errors as learning tools will help you do better next time.

Try this system on your next test, and see if you don't get a better-than-usual grade.

The techniques that will help you get better grades will also help you **clean your room**. Keep it simple by taking a look at what needs doing and taking it apart by task.

1. Collect the trash, dirty clothes, and used sheets.
2. Take the dirty stuff to the laundromat.
3. Put clothes, books, papers, records where they belong.
4. Reorganize your filing cabinet.
5. Wipe the dust and grime off shelves, desk, walls.
6. Clean the windows.
7. Sweep the floor.
8. Rearrange the furniture.

Take away what doesn't need doing (2 and 4, perhaps). Take another look, and put the tasks in order.

If you want to rearrange the furniture, fine, but plan to do that *before* you dust and sweep! Then do each task step by step and one by one: Straighten one corner at a time. . . . Don't start washing one window and then turn to dusting.

Keep your goals in mind: You're really going to please your mom, you're going to be able to find things, and you're aiming to do this by the deadline you've set for yourself. So what are you waiting for? Take off!

Then, when you're part way through and realize you won't have time to finish, back up. Rethink the project, and plan what *must* be done. Do what *can* be done (just straightening?), and give yourself a hand for doing that much.

See? It works! Now in case you're not ready to clean your room or take that exam, here are some exercises to try.

TRY IT!

Get your imagination in gear to apply first aid to the following situations:

What's Missing?
Sally planned a surprise party for Fred. She picked a time and place and sent out invitations well in advance to the list of people she knew he'd enjoy—remembering to warn them to keep it a secret. She knew that Fred had a music lesson every Thursday night, so she arranged to have some of his friends "run into" him outside the teacher's house that night. She made a list of all the party ingredients (food, drinks, paperware, decorations, music), budgeted for them, and got help in gathering them at the right time and place. On the night of the party, everything went according to plan, but the surprise was a fizzle. Why?

(She forgot to check with Fred. He and his family took off for a long weekend that Thursday night.)

What Do You Do First?
You see a woman collapse on the street. She's cut her head and it's bleeding badly, and her arm is bent funny, but she's breathing. Has she broken her arm? Had a heart attack? Will she need a bypass operation? Cosmetic surgery? What do you do?

(Stop the bleeding as best you can, and call for help.)

What's the Point?
In the situation above, what would be your goals?

Long-range: (Save her life.)
Medium-range: (Get help.)
Immediate: (Stop the bleeding.)

In a situation like that, the goal seems clear.

But how about this goal-setting problem: You want to go to the beach with some friends. You've hung onto enough money to do it, found someone to sub at your weekend job, gotten your gear together, and you're all set. It's a beautiful beach day—but your car won't start.

What's your goal now?

(Your goal is still "to go to the beach"—only the "how" of it has changed.)

And another: Ever since opening his first lemonade stand at age eight, Andy has enjoyed the hustle of the business world. Now he's almost out of high school, and he already has two jobs and a savings account for starting his own store someday. Of the following goals, which is/are the most appropriate for Andy?

1. Get outstanding grades
2. Get into the best possible academic college
3. Get a job
4. Get an Army commission
5. Get his high school diploma

(5 and 3)

What's Next?

Ann has done a careful, S–O–S job of applying to colleges: She's taken a look at all the information available to her in the school's catalogs, in the library, and in the counselor's office; taken the information apart to decide what she wants and what she doesn't want, what's possible and what's impossible; and taken away the options that aren't right for her.

She's read all the application instructions carefully and organized herself to get them completed and mailed in an orderly fashion. Step by step, she's filled them out and sent them.

Of the six colleges she applied to, four accepted her, but the one she most wanted put her on the waiting list. Of the four that accepted her, the one she least wanted to attend offered her the most financial aid.

What does she do now?

(Now, it's time to A–C–T. She has to decide which goals are most important to aim for. Should she wait to see whether the school she really wanted accepts her? Should she rethink her goals, take the financial aid, and go to the school she likes least? Should she attend her second-choice school though it will call for more money?)

She balances her priorities and decides to take the third option. *Now* what?

(She has to set new goals and count down her time to earn more money for school.)

What Comes First?

Ben is doing his homework, and he wants a snack: Ice cream sounds good. What does he do first? Finish his homework? Check his wallet? Run to the store to buy ice cream? Check the freezer?

Margie has three hours to go before her party, and everything's set but Margie herself. She hasn't decided what to wear. She's also very grimy, and her hair's a mess. What does she do first? Take a bath? Run to the store to buy a dress? Call one of her friends to borrow some clothes? Check her closet again?

One final, and most important, "to do." Get your pad and pencil and really do these: They're the last step toward the GO process that you've already seen is worth practicing.

Enough of Jessie and Jake, Marilyn and Marvin, Mike and Margie, and all the others. Now it's your turn.

After you've taken a look at the dreams on your GO chart, take your pad and jot down at least one thing that you want to GO for: today, this week, this month, this year, next year, in three years, in five years.

Remembering that goals can be things you want to be, to

become, to accomplish, or to own, write as many GO-for-it goals as you want, but write at least one for each category. Put today's date at the top of the pad so that sometime in the future, you can see how you're doing.

Now, for at least one short-range and one long-range goal, make lists on another sheet of paper of the steps required to reach those goals.

Once you've done that, get going! Put all you've learned and practiced in this book to work for you—toward the goals that *you* want to reach.

But remember. If all plans fail and every step stumbles, if you have too much to do and no time to do it, if you don't know where you're going and have no idea of how to get there—*simplify*.

INDEX